Politics, Policy and Higher Education in India

Sunandan Roy Chowdhury

Politics, Policy and Higher Education in India

palgrave
macmillan

Sunandan Roy Chowdhury
Sampark Global Journal
Kolkata, India

ISBN 978-981-10-5055-8 ISBN 978-981-10-5056-5 (eBook)
DOI 10.1007/978-981-10-5056-5

Library of Congress Control Number: 2017944548

Printed on acid-free paper

This Palgrave Macmillan imprint is published by Springer Nature
The registered company is Springer Nature Singapore Pte Ltd.
The registered company address is: 152 Beach Road, #21-01/04 Gateway East, Singapore 189721, Singapore

For my father Sudeb Roy Chowdhury (1936–2007)
who taught me to reflect on politics
and urged me to value the power of policy

Contents

An Unmitigated Evil

The system of education is an unmitigated evil. I put my best energy to destroy that system. I don't say that we have got as yet any advantage from that system. The advantages we have so far got are in spite of the system, not because of the system. Supposing the English were not here, India would have marched with other parts of the world, and even if it continued under Moghul rule, people would learn English as a language and a literature. The present system enslaves us, without allowing a discriminating use of English literature. My friend had cited the case of Tilak, Ram Mohan and myself. Leave aside my case, I am a miserable pigmy.

Tilak and Ram Mohan would have been far greater men, if they had not the contagion of English learning. I am opposed to make a fetish of English education. I don't hate English education. I don't want to destroy the English language, but read English as an Indian nationalist would do. Ram Mohan and Tilak (leave aside my case) were so many pigmies who had no hold upon the people compared with Chanakya, Shankar, Kabir and Nanak. Ram Mohan and Tilak were pigmies before these giants. What Shankar alone was able to do, the whole army of English-knowing men can't do. I can multiply instances. Was Guru Govind a product of English education? Is there a single English-knowing Indian who is a match for Nanak, the founder of a sect second to none in point of valour and sacrifice?

If that race has ever to be revived, it is to be revived not by English education. I know what treasures I have lost in not knowing Hindustani and Sanskrit. I ask you to consider and value the glamour of education at its true worth. English education has emasculated us, constrained our intellect, and the manner of imparting this education has rendered us effeminate. We want to bask in the sunshine of freedom, but the enslaving system emasculates our nation.

M.K. Gandhi
Young India
April 1921

CHAPTER 1

Introduction

Abstract Introduction provides a curtain raiser for the book. It points out that the book is about higher/tertiary education in India, the functions that the Indian university has played in the specific fashioning of governance, control, and development in India, and that Indian higher education policy is the principal focus area of the book. How politics and policy are enmeshed in the making of higher education in India that is what the book unravels. This chapter gives a sketch of what lies ahead in the book's main five chapters. The author outlines the thrust of each of the chapters from Chaps. 2 to 6, namely, "Brahmin Language, Hindu Growth: Politics and Power of English Language in India," "Western University, Indian Nationalisms," "Cold War to Brand Wars: Global Processes, Developmental Visions, and Indian Higher Education," "Class Struggles in Class Rooms: Conflict, Politics, and the Indian University," and "Elite Institutions, Dismal Development: The Poverty of Indian Higher Education." Here, the author also points to some of the main questions the book addresses, such as does higher education strengthen democracy or does it weaken the democratic and socialist ideals enshrined in Indian Constitution of 1950?

Keywords British colonial rule · Higher/tertiary education in india
Dominant policy prescriptions · India's ideas of development
Injustice in Indian universities · Binary of colonial/national

S. Roy Chowdhury, *Politics, Policy and Higher Education in India*,
DOI 10.1007/978-981-10-5056-5_1

In the last three centuries, India has received, adopted, and adapted important axes to govern, control, and oppress itself. The English language, the specifics of nationalism, Western science including Western medicine, industrial technology, parliamentary democracy, and a juridical system based on England's justice system are key components of modern India. And the Indian variant of Western university is at the core of this constellation of governance, control, and oppression. But language, nationalism, and technology cannot govern, rule, or oppress by themselves. These inanimate tools are used and abused by human beings to govern, rule, and oppress other human beings. While India's colonial rule inaugurated most of these ideas, ideals, and institutions, the specific fashioning of these technologies of governance and development has happened in the heads and hands of Indians themselves. And India was not a blank slate before the inauguration of this Western/colonial set of structures. The pre-existing patterns negotiated with the new thrusts, and this has resulted in a new India where the old lives and thrives with the Western/colonial influence and the more recent post-independence developments.

This book is about higher/tertiary education in India, the functions that the Indian university has played in the specific fashioning of governance, control, and development in India. I am specifically interested here in Indian higher education policy. Who are the policymakers, what are the policy prescriptions, and what do those policy prescriptions tell us about the dominant patterns of Indian thought and the ideas, ideals, and structures that govern India? Who gains from policy, and who loses out, does education/higher education policy lead to social transformative processes, or does it ensure reproduction of social stratification? Do higher education policy and the higher education world work toward greater benefits in health, education, arts, culture, and development of the nation at large or does it work as a self-serving institution for a few that benefits from higher education? Does higher education strengthen democracy or does it weaken the democratic and socialist ideals enshrined in Indian Constitution of 1950?

The roots of this book lie in a one year research project I did in 2002–2003 as a fellow of the International Policy Fellowship (IPF) program of the Open Society Institute (OSI) [part of the Soros Foundations Network] in Budapest. My project was to map the post-university lives of student activists and its impact on society. I studied four universities in four different countries: Ljubljana University in Slovenia, Warsaw

University in Poland, Dhaka University in Bangladesh, and Jawaharlal Nehru University (JNU) in India. I interviewed approximately 15 individuals from each university and told a story of university and social change in each case; it was an exercise in oral history. My project was part of a much larger global study on universities and social transformation, led by the Centre for Higher Education Research and Information (CHERI) of the Open University, UK. Through conferences over a period of a year and half in Europe, Africa, and India, I was exposed to a great variety of resources in higher education research as well as intricacies of policy research. This led me to design a study on Indian higher education policy. At a snail's pace, I wrote a Ph.D. at the Education Department of Delhi University and submitted a thesis in 2011. Of the five chapters of this book, the first and the third specifically draw upon my Ph.D. work.

In "Brahmin Language, Hindu Growth," I look at politics and power of English language in India. I map the contested growth, complexity, and impact of English education in India from India's contact with European Christian missionaries, during the period of colonial rule and in post-1947 independent India. I critique the dominant policy prescriptions and environment that have ensured the growth of English as a new caste marker, a tool of domination and of material enrichment in the hands of a numerically tiny but powerful elite.

"Western University, Indian Nationalisms" is about contrasting nationalisms, their emergence in colonial India, and how nationalisms and universities were tied together in intimate relationships. The idea of India is a contested one. Conceptions of an ideal India inform India's politics and society today, and it did so since and during British colonial rule. As India's educational system and higher education institutions developed in the colonial period, especially after the 1850s, the idea of Indian nation took shape in minds of educated Indians. For 200 years since the early 1810s, higher education institutions have been centers of discourse on nationalism. Various groups of Indians with ideological motivations centered on secularism, Hindu identity, Islamic identity, and women's emancipation have fashioned their versions of Indian nationalism on educational campuses. In some instances, the founding of educational institutions itself has been the result of the specific national vision that the founders had. In short, higher education and contrasting and conflicting versions of nationalism have been enmeshed in India for 200 years. Indian university has been a site of visions of Indian nationalism. I argue that the idea of India that has projected itself most powerfully has done so in great measure in the universities, even before creating the similar impact on the wider public world. I also argue the dominant and dominating idea of Indian nationhood has skillfully elbowed out competing visions of Indian nationalism. However, the different streams of visions continue to jostle for influence in contemporary India today and in its higher education space.

In "Cold War to Brand Wars," I discuss global processes, developmental visions, and Indian higher education. Modern and contemporary India's development and ideas of development are inextricably linked to the policies set in motion during British colonial rule. Indian elites' conception of development was heavily influenced by their exposure to development in Britain and Western Europe. The pattern of the Indian mind to fashion development along Western lines took a new step forward with independence. Post-1947 India was faced with a bipolar world of superpower rivalry between the USA and the USSR. The Cold War impacted India's development, its higher education, and the policy environment. The decades since 1990 have seen the impact of globalization and a new era of world politics. I discuss the impact of global processes on Indian development and higher education policy and narrate the shifts in India's developmental visions. The selective use of science by Indian policy planners, a specific view of the West within dominant Indian opinion and a particular understanding of development, has impacted India's policy in higher education. I argue a narrow and elite-serving view of development has had limiting impact on the growth and flowering of Indian higher education and society.

In "Class Struggles in Classrooms," I discuss the conflict, politics, and the Indian university. In recent years, Indians have woken up in the morning to news of suicides committed by university students from lower-caste/class background; many have happened in elite institutions. What has prompted students from economically depressed and socially marginalized sections of Indian society to commit suicide? Does the malaise stem from and point toward a deep injustice within Indian society? India's universities, especially the ones that are funded by the government, have been founded with the objectives enshrined in Indian Constitution, those of justice, liberty, and equality. The higher education system professes to further the cause of education, enlightenment, freedom, and justice. In reality, the Indian university is a space where injustice continues, on a number of axes of discrimination, such as language, caste, class, gender, urban/rural, and physiological disability. I discuss the social and cultural experience of students from margins of society in the sites of higher education. This chapter also looks into the nature of control and of politics in the higher education space. I argue that instead of having a transformative role, in most part, the Indian university plays a key role in reproduction of the inequities of the Indian social system. And, finally, I point out that this becomes possible because of a poverty of politics in India.

The following chapter, "Elite Institutions, Dismal Development," shows how an undemocratic thrust on elite higher education institutions has led to a dismal state of higher education and development. In the last 25 years, India has experienced reasonably high rate of economic growth, and the purchasing power and size of the middle class have grown. At the same time, the primary health indicators and the basic education indicators of the country have remained poor, in many instances much worse than a poorer economy, that of neighboring Bangladesh. While India is always talked about in the Indian and global press as an important emerging economy, the ground realities of living condition of majority of Indians remain abysmally poor. India plans smart cities while its child mortality rates are higher than that of most its neighbors. India's software industry boasts of providing a wide range of services to global clients while roads in its major cities remain potholed and clogged with traffic; it sends machines into space and its biggest financial hub of Mumbai gets paralyzed with rains every monsoon.

The state of dismal development can be found in the higher education sector as well. Policymakers continually talk about "the crisis" in Indian education; I say, the crisis gets louder by the day. The answer to the flaws lies in what I call a mentality of caste and continuation of a system put in place during the colonial era. I show how an architecture and geography of injustice plagues the nation. Both in the way how university world has been fashioned and especially in the case of disciplines and conceptualization of knowledge, Indian higher education has remained nearly frozen at 1947. I argue, in order to create a robust higher education world, India has to unshackle itself from the mentality of caste and archaic conceptualizations of disciplines. Though I see the flaws of colonial structures, I argue we need to move out of the binary of colonial/national. Educational freedom which leads to a new ordering of disciplines and of higher education holds the key to a just, equitable, dynamic, and sustainable growth in India. A complete conceptual overhaul of Indian higher education alone can lead to a developed India.

The book has been a long time in the making. My interest in politics started at our family dinner table in discussion with my father who filled a little boy with anecdotes from Indian politics. From that early start, I have learnt politics, history, economics, policy, philosophy, education, environment, values, and contested meanings from a great many friends and teachers in different locations in India and abroad. Among the many who have shaped my understanding and stimulated my mind are Basab Bhattacharya, Ajit Chattopadhyay, Swami Girijananda, and Swami Asaktananda in Narendrapur; Subhas Chakraborty, Rajat Kanta Ray, Shirin Masood, Rudrangshu Mukherjee, and Hari Vasudevan in Presidency College; Romila Thapar, Bipan Chandra, Majid Siddiqui, Indivar Kamtekar, Shirin Ratnagar, and Aditya Mukherjee in JNU; Amitabha Choudhury, Gaston Roberge, Ranabir Samaddar, Santanu Chakraborty, Biplab Chakraborty, Saswata Ghosh, and Suvojit Bagchi in Calcutta; Muhammad Yunus, Abdullah Abu Sayeed, Abul Momen, and Mahmud Hasan in Dhaka; DD Nampoothiri and Vinod Krishnan in Kerala; Amy Kazmin, James Lamont, Daniel Lak, Tarun Bose, and Rajib Ray in Delhi; Mohan Kanda in Hyderabad, Yehuda Elkana and Pamela Kilpadi in Budapest; Zmago Smitek, Iztok Osojnik, and Evald Flisar in Slovenia; John Brennan, Yann Lebeau, and Anita Nassar in London; Kian Tajbakhsh in New York; Timothy Ryback in Paris; Ashis Nandy through his books and in lively discussions, Saleem Badat in South Africa; Anna Lindberg and Staffan Lindberg in Sweden; Anne Vihakara in Finland; and Jacob Dreyer and Rex Harrower in free-wheeling discussions in different locations. I did my Ph.D. with Rumesh Chander of the Education Department of Delhi University, without his kindness and generosity I would have been a doctoral drop-out. My father did not live to see this book, nor did my wife Sujatha. My son Chandril, apart from dearly loving his little sister Ananya, has become passionately involved in the practice of education. I hope they and their generation will engage with some of the ideas and ideals that this book throws up.

CHAPTER 2

Brahmin Language, Hindu Growth—Politics and Power of English Language in India

Abstract The use of English in India's everyday lives varies widely. The head of a large business corporation may use a language other than English only when she speaks to her cook or the driver of her car. At the other extreme, a school teacher of science at a Hindi-medium school in a town in the state of Madhya Pradesh may use English only when she has to deal with a physics syllabus that is written in English or if she wants to read education policy documents emanating from government sources or think-tanks in New Delhi. There are a 100 different gradations of the use and power of English in Indian lives within these two ends of the pendulum. Has India always lived with English, have Indians lived with another such language of power other than English, how long have Indians lived with English, and what has English done to Indians, to their minds, to their education, to their culture, to their economic and social development, to their pursuit of knowledge of sciences and humanities, and to India as a civilization? In this chapter, I try to see the contested growth, complexity, and impact of English education in India from India's contact with European Christian missionaries, during the period of colonial rule and in post-1947 independent India. I ask, has English done India good, has it been bad for Indians, can India live without English, and if India cannot live without English, how exactly should India live with English? This chapter is divided into three main parts. The first part "India's British/European Encounter and Indian Higher Education" looks at the development of English and development of the ideas of "development" in India between 1700,

S. Roy Chowdhury, *Politics, Policy and Higher Education in India*,
DOI 10.1007/978-981-10-5056-5_2

when the initial Europe–India encounters began, and 1947, the year of India's independence from British rule. The second "Independence and After—Language, Education, and Development" sees how higher education policymaking in independent India has created and nurtured the power of English as a Brahminical language and what it has meant for the nature of India's economic and educational development. The third part, "Concluding or Continuing the Debate," explores possible alternatives in India's language policy and what that can mean for alternatives in India's politico-economic and edu-cultural spheres of development. A postscript offers policy-relevant actionable suggestions in the area of language and development.

Keywords English education · European knowledge
Brahminical power of English · Underdevelopment of Indian society
Language and development · Empowerment of Indian languages

Indians live with English, Indians who live in India's big, medium, and small cities and in villages, Indians who have been educated in schools where medium of instruction is either one of the Indian languages or in English-medium schools, Indians who are employed as doctors, technocrats, lawyers, bankers, school and university teachers, clerks, bureaucrats, journalists, businesswomen, and politicians. The use of English in India's everyday lives varies widely. The head of a large business corporation may use a language other than English only when she speaks to her cook or the driver of her car. At the other extreme, a school teacher of science at a Hindi-medium school in a town in the state of Madhya Pradesh may use English only when she has to deal with a physics syllabus that is written in English or if she wants to read education policy documents emanating from government sources or think-tanks in New Delhi. On one end of the pendulum is the science teacher in whose life English is nearly absent apart from the source of power that it wields, and on the other end is the CEO in whose life Indian languages other than English are nearly absent, except when they are to be used with service providers who do not have any facility of the English language whatsoever.

Has India always lived with English, have Indians lived with another such language of power other than English, how long have Indians lived with English, and what has English done to Indians, to their minds, to their education, to their culture, to their economic and social development, to their pursuit of knowledge of sciences and humanities, and to India as a civilization? I map the contested growth, complexity, and impact of English education in colonial and post-colonial India.

India's British/European Encounter and Indian Higher Education, 1700–1947

The first saplings of English education in India were planted by Christian missionaries from Denmark. Missionaries from Denmark, Scotland, England, and America started work in eastern and southern India in the early decades of eighteenth century. Their work was centered, among other places, in Madras, Vishakhapatnam, Calcutta, Dhaka, and Bombay. As early as 1716, Danish missionaries started an institution for the training of teachers and, in the next year, two charity schools in Madras. They taught English and principles of Christianity.[1] The missionaries also persuaded local rulers to open English schools in Tanjore, Ramnad, and Sivaganga.

Early Empire Builders Admired Oriental Knowledge and Languages

The year 1757 marks the beginning of the rule of East India Company, first in Bengal and then gradually it spread to other parts of India. In the first decades of the Company's reign, the men at the top were convinced that the "knowledge of the natives of India" in Persian, Arabic, and Sanskrit were important repositories of knowledge, and hence, Indians should be educated in their own languages including their vernaculars.[2] Moreover, they thought and accordingly directed policy that the English men working for the East India Company should learn Persian and one Indian vernacular language.

In this period, Warren Hastings, the Governor General, had suggested the establishment of a professorship of Persian at Oxford. Hastings established the Calcutta madrasa, where Muslim students were taught, so that they could later qualify to hold lucrative offices. The course of study followed the traditional pattern embracing theology, logic, rhetoric, grammar, law, natural philosophy, astronomy, geometry, and arithmetic. Around the same time, John Owen, Chaplain to the Bengal Presidency, requested the Government to establish schools for the teaching of English "to the natives of these provinces."

In 1791, the practice was started of giving writers a monthly allowance for employing a Munshi to teach Persian or an Indian vernacular and promotion depended on knowledge of such a language. In 1794, a rule came into force that starting 1796, no company's servant would be eligible for the office of a Collector unless he showed proficiency in an Indian language.

Wellesley, Governor General for a period starting 1798, wanted to found a college at Fort William,[2] the military–administrative–economic center of the East India Company, comparable to Oxford and Cambridge. This was to be a college for the young British civil servant, who had signed up to serve in the administration of British India. Besides Persian, Arabic, and Sanskrit, six Indian vernaculars were to be taught—Hindustani, Bengali, Telugu, Marathi, Tamil, and Kannada. Muslim and Hindu Laws should be studied as well as English Law, jurisprudence, and the laws enacted by the Governor-General-in-Council. Political economy, world geography, and mathematics were to be offered. The modern languages of Europe as well as Latin, Greek, and the English classics would be provided for. There would be provision for courses in ancient and modern European history and also in the history and antiquities of Hindustan and the Deccan. The grand plan for Fort William College that Wellesley had did not get approval from London. A set of political and economic factors went against Wellesley's vision in higher education. The Fort William College did continue in a pygmy version of Wellesley's vision till 1854.

In debates in British Parliament, the idea of imparting "useful knowledge" to the inhabitants of British India was put forth. But this idea lost out at that time to those who thought the Hindus "had as good a system of faith and morals as most people." The dominant British opinion was of the view that it will be unwise to think of any other education than what people in India already had a tradition of. There was also the thought that Britain had lost America because of its "folly" of allowing the establishment of schools and colleges, and the same "folly" should not be repeated in India.

English, European Sciences, and Useful Knowledge

In early 1800s, Charles Grant, a director of the East India Company, advocated the setting up of English schools which, he argued

> will open to them a world of new ideas ... The Hindus would in time, become teachers of English themselves; and the employment of our language in public business, for which every political reason remains in full force, would, in the course of another generation, make it very general throughout the country. (UEC 1950: 8)

Two successive Governor Generals, Lord Minto and Lord Moira, talked about the need for dissemination of literature and Western sciences among Indians. The well-to-do and educated Indians were also keen to spread European knowledge. In 1817, the Hindu College was created in Calcutta, primarily by the efforts of Bengalis/Indians. School book societies and similar such organizations were being formed by educated and well-to-do Indians in, among other places, Calcutta and Bombay, and the demand for books in English was growing. In 1823, Mountstuart Elphinstone, the governor of Bombay Presidency, urged in a minute, the establishment of schools for teaching English and the European sciences.

From an analysis of the trends and debates in the East India Company, the British Parliament, and the Christian missionaries, three separate strands emerge in educational thinking,[3] namely:

1. India and Indians have knowledge of and in Sanskrit, Persian, and Arabic. That knowledge is of high quality and in no way less than what other cultures/civilizations possess. So, it is fair to continue education and patronize educational systems in such a way that educational development is in these languages and in the knowledge universe of these languages.
2. Introducing the teaching and learning of English is important for the dissemination of Bible and other Christian texts. English will also help create in the "natives" of India better citizen-subjects.
3. English is also the bearer of the European "modern" sciences, and an introduction of English will help the dissemination of "useful" knowledge to Indians.

Sons and Daughters of Macaulay

William Babington Macaulay is a much-maligned man. One of his sentences from his minute of 1835 delivered in the British Parliament has been cited in endless histories and social analytical texts of modern and contemporary India.[4] He had asserted:

> who could deny that a single shelf of a good European Library was worth the whole native literature of India and Arabia.

While the above statement has earned him wrath and scorn of educated Indians, another of his statement has defined the nature of India's modernity and, in a complex inter-relationship, its education. He had said, the aim of English education was to form

> a class of persons, Indian in blood and colour, but English in tastes, in opinions, in morals and in intellect.

It is important to note that even though Macaulay is famous for these words, he conceived an empowerment of Indians wherein Indians may take over the reign of India and British rule could end. The empire of his vision was one of

> pacific triumphs of reason over barbarism: that empire is the imperishable empire of arts and morals, our literature and laws. (UEC 1950: 10)

Taking a cue from Macaulay, Lord Bentinck, then the Governor General, ruled:

> the great object of the British Government in India was henceforth to be the promotion of European literature and science among the natives of India; and that all the funds appropriated for the purpose of education would be best employed on English education alone. (UEC 1950: 11)

This decision of Bentinck was in no less measure influenced by economic exigencies. In 1833, the Charter Act was passed, and at that time, the East India Company was facing a financial crisis. The Governor General wanted to reduce expenditure. One of the major heads of expenditure was the big salaries of English officers. It made eminent sense to add more Indians to the administration at lesser pay. With Macaulay's minute and Lord Bentinck's decision, English and the charm of Anglophone civilization came to stay. India had started to be ruled by the British East India Company after 1757. From 1835, it started to be ruled by the sons and much later by daughters of Macaulay.

Prior to British rule in India, there were long stretches of time when Indian civilization lived with one or the other elite language of power. For centuries, Sanskrit was the language of power/knowledge. Texts were composed in Sanskrit, which remained the preserve of Brahmins, the highest caste of Indians. Brahmins wore a sacred thread to demarcate special status and that they knew Sanskrit. Knowledge of Sanskrit ensured Brahmins' domination of majority of the population while a small ruling class comprising Kshatriyas (the warrior caste) and the Brahmins remained the principal axis of power. During the rule of the Turko-Afghan Sultanate and the Mughal Empire, Persian became the elite language of power. With Macaulay's advocacy and Bentinck's decision, English became the new Brahminical thread of status and power in a new India. It created a new power elite, and English became the central tool of acquiring, retaining, and asserting power for this new Anglophone Brahminical elite.

Conflict and Growth from 1835 to 1947

The 1835 ruling in favor of English led to the popularity of English education all across India. New colleges and schools were set up, quite often under the direct involvement/patronage of wealthy Indians. In 1844, Lord Hardinge declared that English-educated Indians will get priority in all government appointments. That policy continued in matters of governance and rule of power till 1947, the year of India's independence. This policy is visible in the higher echelons of Indian government till today and is an unwritten code in big Indian business corporations and in many small and medium companies too.

But the reach of English education and the appeal of Western civilization did not become universal among Indians. In 1857, a rebellion popularly known as the Sepoy Mutiny broke out. Indian soldiers of the British Indian Army rose up in revolt and a number of Indian rulers joined them and they attempted an overthrow of British rule. The rebellion failed. However, what 1857 shows is that all sections of the Indian population were not great votaries of the English/Western science project of Macaulay, Bentinck, or of Indians like Rammohun Roy who advocated wholesale adoption of English education and civilization. Areas such as Bengal or Bombay, where British rule created a new class of Indians who could profit from the reign, favored the establishment and expansion of English and Western science. At the same time, there were large parts where people did not accept the supremacy of British/ Western economic, military, and cultural power.

Medical, legal, and technological education grew in the nineteenth century—the spread was slow and geographically uneven across India. However, it was a gradual but sure way of extending the hold of English language and European knowledge, and hence British power to all aspects of society and government in India. Between 1818 and 1860, institutions for dissemination of medical learning started in Calcutta, Madras, and Bombay, and engineering education started in Bengal, Bombay, Madras, and United Provinces. In the field of legal education, the teaching of law in this period gave importance to Muslim and Hindu Laws and was practiced in institutions such as the Calcutta madrasa and Banaras Sanskrit College. While the practice and belief in Western technology and medicine have been near total in what is today's middle-class India, law still remains a much-contested terrain. This throws up along with language a challenge to wholesale Westernization.

The policy slant of Macaulay–Bentinck was entirely for English. Subsequent policy documents have a more nuanced approach. The educational dispatch of Sir Charles Wood to the Court of Directors of the Company in 1854, for example, argued that study of Indian languages should be encouraged and English should be taught where there was a demand for it. It goes farther to say that both English and Indian languages should be regarded as the medium for diffusion of European knowledge. The Wood's Dispatch is particularly in favor of using Indian languages for the expansion of mass education.

In spite of such strands of thought, the hegemonic hold of English as well as the awe of European science and civilization grew among affluent and educated Indians, and so did the number of educational institutions imparting English education, especially in the late nineteenth and early twentieth centuries.[5] In the process, it created a new class of educated middle-class Indians. However, this class was principally formed by the upper castes of traditional Indian society. So, while taking advantage of the new Brahminical thread, namely, English, the old Brahminical forces retained their hegemony over Indian society. In the field of language alongside English, languages like Hindi or Urdu developed. Smaller languages like Magahi, Maithili, and Bhojpuri, to name some languages of north India, were marginalized.[6] In terms of caste/class hegemony as well as in domination of a few languages over many, the growth of education and pattern of social change in the second half of nineteenth century and the first half of twentieth-century India retained the domination of small groups over the vast majority of the population.[7] English did not liberate India but it only supplanted an earlier elite/power marker of language/knowledge/power. It helped reinforce the domination of upper-caste/class Indians on Indian politics, economy, education, and society.

While the colonial government and the Indian power elite were strongly in favor of English and Western science, what did Indian scientists have to say about the adoption of English in Indian life and education? Early Indian scientists trained in Western science, as Deepak Kumar (Kumar 1998) tells us, had strong ideas about language, education, and national development.[8] S.C. Chuckerbutty (1824–1874), professor of clinical medicine at Calcutta Medical College between 1854 and 1870, said in 1855:

> Education, in its intellectual sense, means the drawing out, disciplining, strengthening, and refining, the power of the understanding; and no language is more calculated for this work in the present state of our country than English ... It has made us all independent thinkers and some of us independent actors.

In contrast, P.C. Ray, a chemist who founded Bengal Chemicals, one of the early industrial enterprises in eastern India, addressed the convocation in Jamia Milia Islamia in 1923:

> Let us not give merely a purely theoretic and literary education that has unfitted us for the affairs of the world, and made us service hunters, thus inviting to our schools the apellation of gholam-khanas (storehouse of servants). (Kumar 1998)

Ray, unlike Chuckerbutty, believed science should be taught through Bengali and other Indian languages. The opinion of Indians was clearly divided in their attitude toward the use of English language.

The outline of educational policy environment that I have sketched so far shows two trends in terms of attitude toward the English language and Western knowledge. One is the wholesale adoption of English language and Western knowledge. Important exponents of this line of thought are Macaulay and Bentinck among the British and Rammohun Roy, Syed Ahmed Khan, and scientists like S.C. Chuckerbutty among the Indians. The second policy strand is that Western knowledge and education are important but they should be diffused in India through the medium of Indian languages, and in this vision, two twin elements are embedded. One is that one's own language is a source of one's legitimate pride, and the other is that an individual comprehends complex ideas better in one's own language rather than in a foreign tongue. The third strand of educational policy and developmental vision linked to it is that of men like Gandhi. This strand of thinking is heavily disposed against Western scientific and industrial modernity and wants India to find its unique path of development where the self-sufficient Indian village communities can be the center of development.

Of these three strands, the wholesale epistemic and educational adoption of English and Western knowledge system dominated the minds of dominant Indian groups. The use of Indian languages did spread in the primary and secondary levels of education but university-level education remained exclusive preserve of English and the English-educated, who, true to Macaulay's wish, bought his vision and tried hard to become "a class of persons, Indian in blood and color, but English in tastes, in opinions, in morals and in intellect." What Macaulay did not explicitly articulate and may not have envisaged is that this "class of persons" became the new English touting Brahmins of a new India. The English fixation of the upper castes/classes was reinforced by the fact that English opened economic doors. From the school book societies of early 1800s in Calcutta and in Bombay to the growth of English-centric colleges and universities in late nineteenth and twentieth centuries, the educational and cultural power of English was always buttressed by its economic and political power.

This new India, however, remained nearly the same as the old India of Brahminical/upper-caste domination where a tiny minority of 10–15% of the population rules over the vast majority of nearly 85% of the laboring population. The social and political function of oppression and exploitation that was once effectively performed by Sanskrit and knowledge texts in Sanskrit and in a lesser way by Persian in a certain period was now taken over by English and Western knowledge as it came to Indians through the medium of English. The visible and not so visible hold of the Brahminical thread of English on the Indian body politic did not seem to loosen even when the scepter, as Macaulay predicted, had passed from British to Indian hands.

Independence and After—Language, Education, and Development, 1947-2017

In a response to Rabindranath Tagore that appears at the beginning of this book, Gandhi had expressed his firm belief regarding the damage caused by English language to Indian civilization. Tagore himself though critical about the roles of English in Indian society had argued that in spite of problematic influences, English language and Western civilization had done India substantial good. The responses to use of English and roles that English language/civilization played in Indian society have oscillated between two ends of a pendulum, both among the English colonial policymakers/administrators and Indian thought leaders. As Indians fashioned their response to British colonial rule, they tried to either imbibe English or oppose the use of English. Those like Gandhi, who were opposed to the use of English in the civic-cultural life of India, wanted to bring Indian languages to the center of India's educational experience. But even Tagore with whom Gandhi differed was in favor of education through the medium of mother tongue as opposed to education through the medium of English.

What then was the intrinsic difference between the two thought leaders? It was the way they viewed the role of the colonizing English civilization on India and Indian minds. Both saw the ills of the influence of English language and civilization: Tagore was willing to see the positive aspects along with the negative ones, and Gandhi could not see almost anything positive in the influence. With such contrasting worldviews/opinions among India's thought leaders, what role did Indian educational thinkers assign to English in the post-independence period? What roles did they conceive for Indian languages apart from English, and how has the relationship between English and Indian languages developed since 1947, particularly in the realm of higher education?

Policy Thinking in Higher Education After 1947

I have surveyed six major higher education policy documents that were initiated by India's federal government after 1947. The documents bear the imprint of policy thinking in New Delhi and other major urban power centers of independent India; they result from thought cultures of India's English-educated elite who steer India's multi-layered and complex educational, business, and politico-governmental processes. The policy documents that I have analyzed are the reports/recommendations of:

1. University Education Commission (UEC), 1948–1949, chaired by S. Radhakrishnan.
2. Education Commission (EC), 1964–1966, chaired by D.S. Kothari.
3. National Policy on Education (NPE), 1986/1992, initiated by prime minister Rajiv Gandhi and finalized by prime minister P.V. Narasimha Rao.
4. Policy Framework for Reforms in Education (PFRE), 2000, Mukesh Ambani and Kumar Mangalam Birla as conveners.
5. National Knowledge Commission (NKC), 2006–2009, chaired by Sam Pitroda.
6. Committee to Advise on the Renovation and Rejuvenation of Higher Education (CARHE), 2008–2009, chaired by Yashpal.

As with Gandhi and Tagore, the thinking in the policy documents also belongs to various points of the pendulum. No document though is anywhere close to Gandhi's views on English education. Even the UEC coming soon after India's independence struggle led by Gandhi opted for a moderate position vis-à-vis the use of English. It says

> the study of the language and the literature of our mother tongue should occupy the first place in general education. Language incarnates the genius of people which has fashioned it. Every word, every phrase conveys some idea of men and women as they ploughed their fields, tended their homes, built their towns or sailed their ships. We get into the spirit of our people by acquiring control over their language.

UEC looks at Sanskrit, English, and Hindi and, finally, opts for Hindi as the federal language and at the same time emphasizes that Hindi should not claim superiority over regional languages. It urges that educated citizens of India be bilingual and as far as possible, multi-lingual. However, it asserts

> English will have to continue as the medium of federal business till the provinces are ready for the change and the provincial educational institutions have spread the federal language adequately.

It stresses that English is a gateway to the world of knowledge and goes on to add

> Unable to have access to this knowledge, our standards of scholarship would fast deteriorate and our participation in the world movements of thought will become negligible ... in the universities no student should be allowed to take a degree who does not acquire the ability to read with facility and understanding works of English authors. We must take into account our Yugadharma. (trans. Yuga = period, dharma = religion, implies the law of the time)

Clearly, a politics of assertion of English was played out in the earliest higher education policy document of independent India. While UEC accepts the importance of mother tongue, by asserting that without knowledge of English, the standards of scholarship would fast deteriorate and India's participation in the world movements of thought will become negligible; it privileges English. Unwittingly, it also privileges the English-knowing groups of India. Ironically, though India has continued to privilege English in its higher education structures, one cannot say that standards of scholarship have not deteriorated or that India has been able to participate in full measure in the world movements of thought. By asserting "*no student should be allowed to take a degree who does not acquire the ability to read with facility and understanding works of English authors,*" the Commission by one stroke of irresponsible thought crippled the educational futures of millions of Indian young women and men. What this kind of thought structure has resulted is that millions of students go through university education in India, they parrot some words, phrases, and sentences of English, and at the end of their education, they get a degree—which may or may not ensure them a foothold in the job market—and as an end result, they neither have any facility over English nor a mastery of their own mother tongue or an Indian language or for that matter any area of human knowledge.

A decade and a half after UEC, EC (1964–1966) takes stock of the entire Indian education system under the chairmanship of D.S. Kothari and puts forward a comprehensive report and recommendations. While the humanistic bent of Radhakrishnan takes a backseat in EC, the privileging of English and other "international" languages continues, and any clear thrust toward empowerment of Indian languages is absent. It says that a "world language" in addition to English should be taught at university level, and the thrust is for Russian, so much so that the Commission says, without the knowledge of Russian, Ph.D. should not be awarded. Though policymakers looked up to the Soviet model, they unfortunately did not study it closely enough to see that in the Soviet Union, Russian and all the major languages of the USSR were developed greatly and they were the medium of higher education. If Indian policymakers were to understand the developmental success of the then Soviet Union in a more acute manner, then they would have formulated policies to deepen knowledge worlds in the Indian languages rather than think of Russian or English as "world languages."

The silver lining in the EC's report, so far as Indian languages and development are concerned, is that it advocates the translation of works of science and technology from Western languages into major languages of India. The problem, however, is once Russian or English or other "world languages" are privileged by saying that Ph.D. cannot be granted without the knowledge of a particular language, then Indian languages are disempowered to the extent that policy turns them into lame institutions.

In NPE (1986/1992),[9] even though there are some signs of democratization in the form of open universities, the issue of language is overlooked. Policymakers advocate distance and open learning through open universities but they fail to see that unless information and knowledge are made available in Indian languages and in mother tongues of people, access to education will be fraught with serious difficulties, and learning outcomes will be mediocre.

Language, Education, and Development in Twenty-First Century

PFRE (2000) touches on certain significant themes. The authors draw on the experience of South-East Asian countries and try to establish a correlation between greater input in education and the relatively new-found economic prosperity of those nations. The report looks at the concept of human capital and says, "...human capital levels act as a driver of technological innovation. Second, human capital stocks determine the speed of absorption of technology." When discussing education development in other select countries, the authors choose Sweden, South Korea, Singapore, Thailand, and China, and from experiences of these countries, they draw lessons and urge

> Creative and independent thinking must be emphasized across the education system in order to promote a learning society.

What is the relation between technology and language? How does education in one's mother tongue or natural language affect development/absorption of new technology? This critically important theme escapes the attention of the authors.

PFRE rightly points out the influence of input in education on the economic prosperity of South-East Asian nations but overlooks the role of culturally sensitive education policy. In most countries of South-East and East Asia, the greatest proportion of education is imparted in the mother tongue. The bearing of language policy on economic/developmental outcomes can be seen in India too. Among young Indians working in the software industry, a large number have not had the privilege of an English-medium education during their school years. They would have usually had difficulty in finding a middle or top management job at an FMCG company but have not faced that cultural hurdle in getting a job in a software firm.

Talking about the introduction of humanistic disciplines in premier technology and management institutes, CARHE (2008–2009) says

> We can then look forward to the day when IITs and IIMs would be producing scholars in literature, linguistics and politics along with engineering and management wizards who would have substantial motivation for engagement with the local community, and the opportunity to use and

> enhance learning by solving real-life problems in their immediate environment.

The authors do not ask, in which language shall technocrats and sociocrats interact with the local community. Won't they require to communicate in Tamil, Telugu or Maithili, or Manipuri to understand the lives and cultures—technological and humanistic of the communities? Won't there be a chasm between the Anglophone higher education they have received and revered and the worlds where the natural language is anything but English.

The language issue plays a key role when we look at the stigmatization of vocational education. CARHE says that majority of students who go to vocational institutions are pass outs of uninspiring schools. What exactly are uninspiring schools? These are government schools in desolate villages, in urban slums, or in lower-middle-class neighborhoods in the cities and towns of India—an extremely large proportion of these schools teach, not in English but in a language which I call the natural language of the region.[10] A great irony of India is that possibly not even 1% of India's top government servants send their children to government-run schools. Stigmatization is rooted in the use of the medium of instruction and the society's perception about Indian languages and English. The primacy given to English leads to a disproportionate power of English and the English-knowing classes of India. The attitude stems from the mentality of Brahminism rooted in Indian minds. Hence be it the introduction of humanistic disciplines and nurturing of socially relevant education in IITs and IIMs or be it the de-stigmatization of vocational education, the answer to a variety of problems plaguing Indian higher education lies in the language question.

On the issue of language, NKC (2006–2009) says

> An understanding and command over the English language is a most important determinant of access to higher education, employment possibilities and social opportunities. School-leavers who are not adequately trained in English as a language are always at a handicap in the world of higher education. More often than not, teaching is in English. Even if it is not, in most subjects, books and journals are available only in English. And those who do not know English well enough find it exceedingly difficult to compete for a place in our premier educational institutions. This

> disadvantage is accentuated further in the world of work, not only in professional occupations but also in white-collar occupations overall.

Pointing to this reality NKC says

> There is an irony in the situation. English has been part of our education system for more than a century. Yet English is beyond the reach of most of our young people, which makes for highly unequal access. Indeed, even now, *no more than one per cent* (italics mine) of our people use it as a second language, let alone a first language.

The strategy of introducing English at the very early stages of education and also giving a thrust to translation may prove to be a sound policy for furthering growth, quality, and research in the higher education sector. The report says

> Translation activities should be seen in tandem with the plan to increase access to English language training across the population, and the promotion of English in school education at the primary level. Both are aspects of the goal of increasing access to knowledge.

Laying emphasis on translation, it says

> Language should not act as a barrier in science teaching. To bring such students to level playing ground, apart from English language lessons, there is a need to arrange speedy and widespread dissemination of basic science education materials in local languages. These courses should be designed to facilitate understanding of fundamental concepts in the local languages and also provide a bridge towards subsequent studies in the English language. Resources should be provided to translate the best science books in local languages. Internet dissemination of these translated books should be carried out.

Clearly, NKC consistently advocated a progressive democratic policy in relation to language. That this becomes all the more important in science teaching goes without saying. It discusses the important theme of the special needs of tribal children, where it says

> Early childhood education is very important as the brain develops the fastest up till six years of age. In this context, special teaching aids need to

> be developed for tribal children as they are not exposed to modern technology like rest of the children. Motivation for learning has to be created by providing exposure to scientific developments. Tribal schools should be equipped with teachers who are trained in pedagogical methods suited to special needs of tribal kids. They should be well versed in local tribal dialect. Science subjects should be taught in local language till mid-school level. However, the teacher should explain fundamental concepts in tribal dialect to ensure sound conceptual understanding. Tribal dialect can be used for evaluation purposes too at lower levels. Nutritional requirements of tribal children should be taken care of.

The opportunity for tribal kids to learn sciences in their own tongues till middle school level will have a positive impact on their educational achievements.

NKC has unequivocally put thrust on education through mother tongue and at all levels—starting with the primary school and going up to higher education, as also of providing education to tribal populations in their own languages. And it has laid stress on the urgent need of translations of scientific and technological literature including textbooks to be made available in Indian languages.

Probably, the most important theme that NKC touched upon is the issue of absorption and fluent use of English in Indian society. It says and I reiterate:

> Indeed, even now, *no more than one per cent* (italics mine) of our people use it as a second language, let alone a first language.

In my view, this is a key to the understanding of the underdevelopment of Indian society. When we are talking of vocational education, national skills mission, and development of skills, more students in science and maths, focus on research-oriented learning, bridging the needs of society with higher education, making education more socially relevant, and making learning–teaching experience a joy for the teacher and the learner—in all of this and in the entire gamut of issues that concern education and development, the key to underdevelopment and the key to the future possibility of meaningful equitable and excellence-centric development lie in the domain of language. As long as Indians are starry-eyed about English, a small number (1–5%) of Indians will use the tool of English to aggrandize themselves and continue an unethical rule of cultural–economic power over the vast majority of Indians. Only with widespread adoption of Indian languages in education systems, empowerment of Indian languages through availability of world-class translations of world knowledge and the marriage of developed grasp of one's own language and foreign languages such as English (and not English alone) with scientific rigor can lead to a developed educational system, a dynamic yet sustainable economy, and a peaceful yet vibrant society in India.

Concluding or Continuing the Debate

Language and education are enmeshed intimately. The geo-cultural mosaic of India is a treasure house of languages. India's people spoke in a variety of languages and educated their young through the millennia. During centralized regimes, the trend was toward the use of a language of power. Persian was the court language and hence the language of the elite in the Mughal era. In the British colonial period, English became the language of government and of the new elite. The colonial period is witness to battle of ideas over language policy. While initial British policy favored continuity of the study of traditional Indian languages such as Persian and Sanskrit and the knowledge worlds of those languages, later, from 1835 onward, with the policy of Macaulay and Bentinck, English became the favored language. Later, the importance of education in vernacular languages, along with English, was stressed, both by colonial policy documents such as the educational dispatch of Sir Charles Wood in 1855 as well as by Indian nationalist leaders and educationists in the late nineteenth and twentieth centuries.

In the post-1947 policy documents, the thinking on language policy has multiple strands, and there is a lack of a clear policy statement on language. The documents stress generally that in primary and secondary education, the child's mother tongue or the language of the particular region should be the medium of instruction. There is a near unanimity that English should be taught but it is usually never stressed that English should be the medium of instruction. However, for the post-secondary, i.e., higher education levels, it is an unsaid unanimity that English should be the preferred medium of instruction. EC (1964–1966) stresses the need of learning additional world languages like Russian at the Masters and Ph.D. level, but that is more an exception reflecting the impact of Cold War politics rather than a general trend.

In the context outlined above, two principal questions arise. Policy thinkers have known that private English-medium schools exist in the big and medium cities of India, for the children of middle classes and the rich. Why do not India's policy thinkers discuss this hiatus between private schools and government ones? Second, how can one expect a smooth switch for millions of young minds from a Bengali-/Malayalam-/Hindi-medium education to an English-medium one at the post-secondary/higher education level? Most policy documents have not explored in detail the reality of English being unable to penetrate into 90% of the Indian population. For the large mass of individuals who have a "basic" knowledge of English, English is not their language. Reports like the NKC give a pointer to the extremely limited use of English in India. The role of Indian languages other than English in higher education is not made clear, and the relationship between development of India's languages and the nation's research capacity, innovation and economic development, is not discussed. Certain policy documents talk about a thrust toward translation and while that is welcome, a roadmap outlining translation's role in creating a research environment in languages other than English is not charted. The possibility of Indian languages becoming homes of scientific and social scientific universes is not even considered. In an absence of a specific roadmap of development of Indian languages and higher education in Indian languages to levels comparable in English, German, or Japanese, India's education policymakers are content to keep its languages, at least the state of social scientific and scientific research and education in these languages, at pigmy levels. Indians who know English and can express their innovative ideas in English have been less than 10% of the educated population in the last 200 years. It will require a miracle whereby the "trickle-down" effect of English learning and knowledge will change this situation in the next 200 years. With Indian languages at pigmy levels, no wonder that India's scientific and social scientific research will remain at pigmy levels too.

In an essay[11] on the state of languages in the intellectual communities of India, Ramachandra Guha (2009) has discussed the decline of bilingual intellectuals, people who were or are equally at intellectual home in English and their mother tongue or one of India's numerous languages. This world of bilingualism and multiculturalism was a result of the Europe–India interface; it never became a large proportion of the population, but it had substantial adherents. As Guha rightly points out, with their differences over the role of English notwithstanding, Tagore and Gandhi were the greatest names among India's bilingual intellectuals. Yet, this intellectual–cultural species born and nurtured in the creative tension of the colonizer and the colonized is dying a slow death. Independent India's education, administration, business, and culture policies in respect to language have not encouraged bilingualism or intellectual/academic linguistic pluralism. The largely unitary state has spawned its centralized and centralizing English-believing elite, thereby creating an ever widening gulf of academic and cultural power between the English-metropolitan and the Indian-language moffusil.

The policy choice before India today as it was at the time of independence is whether the power stream of Indians continue pampering English and those who know English and make do with the country's vast non-English world only to the extent that democracy and majoritarian politics forces upon this power stream, or does India take specific measures to build broad-based deep intellectual homes in its main languages. If India decides to follow the route followed so far since the minute of Macaulay, India will continue to have a small elite that knows English and large sections of population in a permanent state of inferiority complex vis-à-vis English. It will also mean India remains a permanent importer of new technologies. On the contrary, if it makes a break with the policy past and decides to build scientific and intellectual homes in each of India's 20 main languages, then there could be a flowering of research and innovation in these languages taking India's total research output to a substantially high level. The thrust of building intellectual homes in the languages will also lead to a greater success in fields such as social planning, thereby benefitting the working of panchayats, municipalities, and the social sector as a whole.

In recent years, one hears industry leaders moan the lack of an adequate number of skilled workers such as plumbers and electricians. The lack of availability of scientific and technological literature and the overarching educational pattern of English dependence contribute to the poor state of skills education in the country. On the one hand, there is the Brahminical power of English, and on the other hand, the Brahminical mindset of looking down upon labor. These two coupled together to create a neglected and stigmatized environment for an important sector of technical education that does not carry the elite "IIT" (Indian Institute of Technology) tag. As a result, be it in core strength of skilled manpower for engineering and manufacturing sectors, or be it in the quality of service delivery by the medical establishment, India languishes at the near bottom of world tables. The Brahminic use of language power goes hand in hand with the Brahminical anti-labor mindset, resulting in a severe handicap toward creating an industrial economy and a progressive society with reasonable welfare for all. The domination of the Brahmin language called English and the accompanying stigmatization of labor and laboring people contribute to the politico-economic and edu-cultural architecture of Hindu growth.

A radical break in language policy at the higher education level can usher in changes that will lead to a different India. This change where Indian languages become the intellectual home of scientists and social scientists will take decades if not a century. When it happens, the forces of language democracy will most likely unleash a scientific revolution in each language leading to a renaissance and scientific flowering in Indian civilization. Falling short of such a revolution, India as a nation/civilization will have to remain content with its roles as clerks, cyber-accountants, and call center operators. For that, of course, English can serve India well.

Postscript: Brahmin Language, Dalit Politics

My thoughts on English, its power, and domination in independent India have evoked mixed responses. After a lecture, listeners in the audience would ask/say:

- Were it not for English, could India remain a united republic?
- If you wanted to remove English, then Hindi would take over and that would be disastrous.
- The only way to remove social/cultural differences in India is to give Dalits and oppressed groups the advantage of English.

Let me look at the power of English once again and try and address these themes. Robert D. King, who carefully examined and documented how Nehru crafted an astute policy in the contested world of politics of language in India, writes

> If India had had the bad luck to have been led at its birth either by an English-hater resolved to rid the land of the English language at all costs or by a weakling not firm about the retention of English, then we should

> have today an India isolated from much of what is good and useful in a world where English has become the international language. Today's India would be an inward dwelling, neurotic backwater. More than likely we should not be speaking of a single India at all, if English had been eliminated, for Dravidian India would not have tolerated second-class linguistic status .... (King 1997)

Gyanendra Pandey (2016) quotes Dalit activist and intellectual Chanderbhan Prasad. Prasad believes:

> There is something mysterious about English, ... English produces the symmetry between brain and the mind .... Tiny minority [of] English nations are the greatest producers of modern knowledge.
>
> If your child learns English as if he or she has inherited 100 acres of land.

Let me start with the Hindi/English theme. When I critique the use and abuse of English in the realm of education, contemporary culture, or higher education policy, I do not propose that English as a connecting language for India be replaced by Hindi. I do not advocate that Hindi engulfs the languages of south India or tramples the many languages of tribal populations in India's northeast and those in the heartland of central India. We have witnessed how Pakistan broke up in 1971, and the imperialism of Urdu on Bengali contributed to the birth of Bangladesh in great measure. So, I am not suggesting Hindi/Urdu imperialism replaces the empire of English. Let English continue as a link language within the many peoples of India, let it also continue to be the principal language for international communication.

But, and this is where I diverge from the dominant trend since 1947, let English and English-knowing minority not have the power to trample over the economic and cultural aspirations of the non-English-knowing majority. If India regards English as vital, it must realize that the Indian languages are even more vital. And India's many languages are vital not only for matters of heart, not only for the "soft" areas of emotion and culture, but even more so for the "hard" areas of business and technology and material and human development. There are some excellent successes which can be seen as example of the cultural-business order I advocate. The Telugu film industry regularly churns out films which are invariably dubbed in Hindi and released in Hindi. The Telugu film industry has grown enormously, and it has profited from the business of dubbing its films in Hindi. This has happened outside the English gaze. At the same time, Hindi did not destroy Telugu; on the contrary, Telugu has profited from Hindi's pan-India reach.

I mentioned the birth of Bangladesh in 1971. How has Bangladesh fared compared to India or Pakistan, state-systems which live under a monster called Anglopolis.[12] Bangladesh is a society and state where nearly 98% of its people work in and with Bengali, the natural tongue of the land. Writing after two decades of India's strong economic growth, Amartya Sen and Jean Dreze (2011) tell us that in spite of high rate of economic growth, India lags behind Bangladesh on all basic health indicators and on a large number of primary and secondary education indicators. Sen and Dreze do not bring in the language angle to this contrast. I think that a major reason behind Bangladesh's better performance is that the policy planner and the bureaucrat in Dhaka speak and write the same language as the village school teacher in a remote district or the small peasant's daughter who aspires to be a management executive in Dhaka or Chittagong. In India itself, the state of Kerala has performed exceedingly well in the area of human development. In the case of Kerala too, I feel that language has played a key role in ensuring greater human development index. Malayalam, the natural language of the state, is a language of both the elite and the people. Once again, a caveat, I am not saying the success of human development in Kerala or in Bangladesh is only for the language question, but I think language plays a key role in the development or underdevelopment of societies.

The idea prevalent among Dalit or Brahmin intellectuals that English nations are great producers of knowledge or that they are more developed societies does not hold water. In the nineteenth century, German was the main language in which the world of physics developed. French and several other European languages have been and still are languages of scientific enquiry. The economic development of Japan, Korea, and China where English is not the national language of power is way ahead of South Asia or sub-Saharan Africa where the power of the local English-knowing elites tramples the vast majority.

As for the Dalit espousal of English, I see Chanderbhan Prasad's point that if a Dalit person learns English, she/he will feel empowered. And I think that Dalits and all historically backward communities should and even must learn English. Knowledge and command over English will definitely empower the Dalit individual. But will learning of English end class/caste domination? No, it will not. Power and those in power act in a complex manner; there are sophisticated tools that the powerful use. If you bridge the language divide, there will be accent divide; if you bridge the education gap, there will be digital divide; English is one of the pillars of the elite club, not the only one. What is central to reduce Brahminical/upper-caste domination is to rob Brahminism of the idea world that validates its power. Let each Dalit individual learn English and learn English well. But let her not lose the language into which she was born. Let her develop a mastery of that language at least as much she masters English. The more pressing question is to purge Indian languages like Bengali, Tamil, Malayalam, Marathi, or Hindi of their inherent authoritarian/hierarchical structures. Disbanding India's languages which are languages both of Dalits and of upper castes, and of upper-caste dominations, will not be an astute decision. It is urgent for Dalits to learn English, but it is even more urgent for Dalit politics to take the contestation into the realm within Indian languages, and to contribute to the greater struggle for "annihilation of caste."

Notes

1. For information on the early beginnings of English education and for a history of education in colonial India, see University Education Commission (1950).
2. While in colonial India, languages spoken by ordinary Indians were referred to as vernaculars, in contemporary Indian parlance, Indian languages spoken by the large mass of people is referred to as regional languages. In the politics of languages, Tamil, Gujarati, and Bengali are referred to as regional languages while English is referred to as national language.
3. For the East India Company's educational policies, see Basu (1982a, b).
4. For an exposition of Macaulay's minute in the British Parliament and his ideas, see University Education Commission (1950).
5. For a history of educational development in this period, see Basu (1974).
6. For an insightful discussion on how Hindi marginalized smaller languages, see Bhokta (1998).
7. For the domination of new class and how the old high caste groupings metamorphosed into a new class, see Barra (1998).
8. For ideas of Bengali scientists like S.C. Chuckerbutty and P.C. Ray, see Kumar (1998).

9. This particular National Policy on Education was first declared in 1986 when Rajiv Gandhi was prime minister. However, it underwent changes both during the period when V.P. Singh was prime minister and when P.V. Narasimha Rao was prime minister. The final text of the document that we have now is a revised text declared in 1992 when P.V. Narasimha Rao was prime minister. Hence, I refer to this document as NPE 1986/1992.
10. For a child whose parents are both native to the Malayalam language, her mother tongue is Malayalam. However, if she grows up from a very early age in Amritsar, a city in Punjab, I think Punjabi becomes her natural tongue, and it is in that language she feels most comfortable.
11. See Guha (2009).
12. I have discussed in an article the dominant and the undemocratic power of English in India and more widely in the Indian sub-continent. See Roy Chowdhury (2014).

Recommended Readings

Government Reports/Policy Documents

Education Commission. 1970. *Education and National Development: Report of the Education Commission (EC)*. New Delhi: NCERT.

Ministry of Human Resources Development. 1992. *National Policy on Education 1986—Programme on Action 1992 (NPE)*. New Delhi: Government of India.

Ministry of Human Resources Development. 2010. *Report of Committee to Advise on the Renovation and Rejuvenation of Higher Education (CARHE)*. New Delhi: Government of India.

National Knowledge Commission. 2009. *National Knowledge Commission—Report to the Nation (NKC)*. New Delhi.

Prime Minister's Council on Trade and Industry. 2000. *Report on A Policy Framework for Reforms in Education (PFRE)*. New Delhi: Government of India.

University Education Commission. 1950. *Report of the University Education Commission (UEC)*. New Delhi: Government of India.

Books/Articles/Essays

Barra, Joseph. 1998. Colonialism and Educational Fragmentation in India. In Bhattacharya.

Basu, Aparna. 1974. *The Growth of Education and Political Development in India, 1898–1920*. New Delhi: Oxford University Press.

Basu, Aparna. 1982a. *Essays in the History of Indian Education*. New Delhi: Concept.

Basu, Aparna. 1982b. Education of Civil Servants during the Company Period. In *Essays in the History of Indian Education*. New Delhi: Concept.

Bhattacharya, Sabyasachi (ed.). 1998. *The Contested Terrain: Perspectives on Education in India*. New Delhi: Orient Longman.

Bhokta, Naresh Prasad. 1998. Marginalisation of Popular Languages and Growth of Sectarian Education in Colonial India. In Bhattacharya.

Dreze, Jean and Sen, Amartya. 2011. Putting Growth In Its Place. *Outlook*, 14 November 2011. https://www.outlookindia.com/magazine/story/putting-growth-in-its-place/278843.

Guha, Ramachandra. 2009. The Rise and Fall of the Bilingual Intellectual. *Economic and Political Weekly* 44 (33): 36–42.

King, Robert D. 1997. *Nehru and the Language Politics of India*. New Delhi: Oxford University Press.

Kumar, Deepak. 1998. Educational Ideas of Bengali Scientists from 1850 to 1920. In Bhattacharya.

Pandey, Gyanendra. 2016. Dreaming in English. *Economic and Political Weekly* 51 (16): 56–62.

Roy Chowdhury, Sunandan. 2014. Monster Anglopolis. *Planet—The Welsh Internationalist*, 216.

CHAPTER 3

Western University, Indian Nationalisms

Abstract "Western University, Indian Nationalisms" is about contrasting nationalisms, their emergence in colonial India, and how nationalisms and universities were tied together in intimate relationships. The idea of India is a contested one. Conceptions of an ideal India inform India's politics and society today, and it did so during British colonial rule. As India's educational system and higher education institutions developed in the colonial period, especially after the 1850s, the idea of Indian nation took shape in minds of educated Indians. For 200 years since the early 1810s, higher education institutions have been centers of discourse on nationalism. Various groups of Indians with ideological motivations centered on secularism, Hindu identity, Islamic identity, and women's emancipation have fashioned their versions of Indian nationalism on educational campuses. In some instances, the founding of educational institutions itself has been the result of the specific national vision that the founders had. In short, higher education and contrasting and conflicting versions of nationalism have been enmeshed in India for 200 years; the creation of the two nation-states of India and Pakistan in 1947 bears testimony to this. Indian university has been a site of visions of Indian nationalism. The idea of India that has projected itself most powerfully has done so in great measure in the universities, even before creating a similar impact on the wider public world. This chapter argues the dominant and dominating idea of Indian nationhood has skillfully elbowed out competing educational visions and of nationalism as was conceived in Vishwa Bharati and Jamia Millia Islamia. Different streams

S. Roy Chowdhury, *Politics, Policy and Higher Education in India*,
DOI 10.1007/978-981-10-5056-5_3

of visions continue to jostle for influence in contemporary India today and in its higher education space.

Keywords Contrasting nationalisms · National education
Oppressiveness of colonial education · Religio-cultural worlds
Educational universes · Non-Eurocentric universalism

English became the new Brahminical thread in nineteenth-century India. It also created an intricately woven cloth, a fabric called English/Western education. The upper castes/classes of India adopted and adapted to the world of Western/English education. Much of this adoption/adaptation happened within the walls of the university, an institution that became the dominant face of Indian higher education in the second half of nineteenth century. While the upper castes/classes from different cultural worlds within India found in the British/Western university the model institution for higher education, the nature of national ideal that universities in colonial India fashioned differed widely. The visions of what higher education institutions meant and what their educational and political/social/cultural ideals were varied from one cultural community to another and from one founder to the other. The Western university in the political/cultural space of colonial India spawned Hindu nationalism, Indian nationalism dominated by Brahminical upper castes/classes, Muslim Indian nationalism, and religio-spiritual universalism of different kinds.

One of the earliest seats of Western learning/teaching in colonial India was the Hindu College, which started in the second decade of nineteenth century in Calcutta. True to its name, for several decades, it remained a Hindu and I would add a Brahminical upper-caste/class institution. Later, the Hindu College was closed down and was replaced by Presidency College,[1] which in principle was open to students and teachers of all communities of India. While the colonial government set up a few universities in the second half of the nineteenth century, notably the ones in Calcutta, Bombay, Madras, and Allahabad,[2] the Indian upper castes/classes also took the lead in setting up educational institutions in the late nineteenth and early twentieth centuries. Some of the prominent institutions set up by elite Indians were the Muhammedan Anglo-Oriental College in Aligarh (later named as Aligarh Muslim University [AMU]), the Banaras Hindu University in Banaras, the Osmania

University in Hyderabad, the SNDT Women's University in Pune, the Viswa Bharati in Santiniketan close to Calcutta, and the Jamia Millia Islamia in Aligarh and later in Delhi.

When the Hindu College was set up in Calcutta in 1817, it reflected the desire of the local Bengali upper-caste elite to be educated in English and in modern Western sciences. Several decades later when Sir Syed Ahmed Khan founded the Muhammedan Anglo-Oriental College in Aligarh, he too believed that knowledge of English and Western science was crucial for Muslims in north India for their development and for gaining leadership positions in society. All of nineteenth century, the dominant classes of Indian society—apart from a section of the traditional elite during the Sepoy Mutiny of 1857—felt English and modern Western science were the keys to India's development. The hegemony of this specific strand of educational/cultural thought of colonial rule held sway over upper-class/caste Indian minds.

Politics Takes Hold

As the nineteenth century rolled into the twentieth, this hegemony did not remain unquestioned. The first half of the twentieth century is a phase of national awakening of India and Indians. It took shape in different nationalisms. Universities played a key role in shaping the many nationalisms of British India. Mushirul Hasan (1998a) paints a vivid picture of AMU and its intimate linkages to Muslim Indian nationalism that finally gave shape to the formation of Pakistan. The loyalty to British rule ingrained in the educational thought of Sir Syed, the founder of the institution, was contested in the twentieth century. Students became politically active in the early decades. Through the 1920s and 1930s, the political environment in AMU witnessed diverse allegiances. There were staunch supporters of the Indian National Congress under the leadership of Gandhi, there were socialists, and also those who were with the Communist Party of India (CPI). Yet gradually, the political force that gained ground and finally triumphed was the ideology of Pakistan, one that believed the Muslims of the sub-continent could only prosper peacefully if they could found a separate nation-state for Indian Muslims. As Muhammad Ali Jinnah believed and made others believe, Hindus and Muslims were two distinct nations. AMU was the battleground of this clash of nationalisms[3]; the whole world of Indian higher education too was a site of this clash where no one nationalism could triumph over another, and where the voices of universalism remained a faint murmur.

AMU's role in the creation of Pakistan can be gleamed from scores if not hundreds of accounts. Hasan quotes the Aga Khan:

> often in civilised history a university has supplied the springboard for a nation's intellectual and spiritual renaissance ... Aligarh is no exception to this rule. But we may claim with pride that Aligarh was the product of our own efforts and of no outside benevolence, and surely it may also be claimed that the independent, sovereign nation of Pakistan was born in the Muslim University of Aligarh. (Hasan 1998a: 191)

Aligarh, which I tend to use interchangeably for AMU, did not reach the Pakistan moment from its very inception. During the first few decades, it was assiduous with the colonial administration and ideology. Even Gandhi was at first rebuffed by the university's students when he gave a call for non-cooperation with the British in 1920. Later though, in the 1920s and most of the 1930s, the Congress under Gandhi's leadership had a big following in Aligarh. The communists too organized a major students' strike in 1936, and the communist All India Students Front (AISF) tried to prevent the setting up of a branch of All India Muslim Students' Federation (AIMSF) in Aligarh; there were students who did not want a Muslim organization in the university where majority of students and teachers were Muslims. But in later 1930s, the tide turned in favor of Muslim nationalism, the Pakistan movement and for its sole spokesman, namely, Muhammad Ali Jinnah. While overt manifestations of aggressive Hindu nationalism in north India, especially in the then United Provinces, could have contributed to the popularity of the Muslim League and the call for Pakistan among Muslim students, students aligned with the Muslim League and their political mentors on campus aggressively put down any opposition to the idea of Pakistan. In the mid 1940s and in the run up to partition/independence in 1947, communist students clashed with the Muslim Leaguers but the die had already been cast; a separate nation-state for Indian Muslims was only a few months away. From allegiance to British crown and English/Western modernity to Gandhian ideals of anti-colonialism to communist worldview of politics of the economically oppressed to Jinnah's idea of two-nation theory that divided Hindus and Muslims, Aligarh had come a long way.

National Education

Muslim Indian nationalism was one of the different nationalisms in colonial India. The cultural assertiveness of Hindu world could be felt in the pattern of politics practiced within the Indian National Congress. Indian nationalism of which Congress under Gandhi became the lead bearer was in a continuous engagement with education. In the politics of nationalism, ideas of "national education" played an important role.

In late nineteenth century, Indians with English education became assertive in the political life of society. Indian National Congress, formed in 1885, was a platform of educated Indians to express their views about the governance of the British Raj. The colonial government's decision to partition Bengal in 1905 spurred a "nationalist" movement in Bengal and beyond—it was popularly known as Swadeshi movement.[4] At this time, the Congress also put forward its thought in educational matters. A resolution on "national education" was adopted at the Congress session held in Calcutta in 1906. It felt it was time people all over the country take up the question of "national education" for boys and girls, and "organize a system of education, literary, scientific and technical, suited to the requirements of the country, on national lines under national control." The themes that came up in this resolution were as follows: Indian/nationalist control, fostering patriotism, provision for religious instruction, no servile imitation of the West, teaching through modern Indian languages, lower fees, and education for boys and girls.[5]

In the "nationalist" phase of modern India, many more educational visions were articulated. In 1937, Gandhi propounded the idea of *Buniyadi talim* or "basic education," also referred to as the Wardha scheme of education. With Gandhi's philosophy as the backbone, it was Zakir Hussain, a future Vice-Chancellor of the AMU after partition, who drafted the policy of *Buniyadi talim*. This bore the hallmarks of Gandhi's political and philosophical vision with a stress on manual work and the importance of linking education to the realities of rural India. Apart from the stress of learning through the medium of Indian languages, the thrust was toward an India that could be idealized through its self-sufficient village republics.[6] While the incorporation of manual work in education was Gandhi's way of countering anti-labor Brahminical mindset of upper-caste Indians, the effort to make education linked to rural realities was his idea of creating a society divested of the "ills" of Western/modern industrialism.

NATIONALISM OF INDIAN SCIENTISTS

Gandhi was vocal in his opinion against adoption of Western science and industry in India. On the other end of the pendulum from him were Indian scientists, men of science who were immersed in Western science and believed in the "scientific project." Early Indian scientists trained in Western science, as we learn from Deepak Kumar (1998), had strong ideas about education and national development. S.C. Chuckerbutty (1824–1874), professor of clinical medicine at Calcutta Medical College between 1854 and 1870, proposed a scheme of "national education." In 1869, Mahendralal Sarkar, also a doctor by training and profession, argued for a "national institution" for the cultivation of sciences by "the natives of India," entirely under Indian management and control. In 1886, P.N. Bose, a scientist at the Geological Survey of India, wrote a pamphlet on technical and scientific education in Bengal and, a decade later, published three volumes titled "A History of Hindu Civilisation." Kumar sees this as a case where "fierce nationalism transformed a geologist into a historian." Bose argued that teaching of science should be linked to the process of industrialization. He advocated India to follow the Japanese path of industrialization and modernization. P.C. Ray a scientist and a pioneering entrepreneur wrote "A History of Hindu Chemistry." Clearly, Indian scientists were fuelled with the idea of nationalism, and in their minds, the greatness of Hindu civilization fed into the stream of Indian nationalism. On the one hand, they urged their fellow Indians to embrace science, and on the other hand, they tried to instill legitimate pride in Indians with the idea that India had a history of science even before India's encounter with modern West. Gandhi's ideals and the ideas of scientists jostled with one another in the shaping of linkages between education and Indian nationalism.

When Indian nationalists think of "national education," their political demand is focused on nationalist control of education. There is no great divergence between nationalists and colonial rulers in the meanings and purpose of education. Krishna Kumar (1991) has pointed to the homonymy in colonialist and nationalist ideas of education. The tiny elite that university education created in colonial India was paternalistic toward the large mass of ordinary Indians, as was the colonial administration. But the homonymy did not stop here. Whether in the issue of use of Indian languages or in the content of courses, nationalists—apart from a few exceptions—did not diverge much from the colonial thinking in education. In an enmeshed relationship with education/higher education, the national movement unleashed processes of social reform but the content of education did not differ greatly from the colonial planning of education. The nationalist movement and expanding educational opportunities opened doors for socially oppressed groups such as the lower and backward castes and women to come forward and be part of an expanding national awakening and freedom struggle. Nationalism as an ideology took education to a wider section of Indian society. This widening social base of education did not, however, take away the elite domination of Indian nationalism. A few thousand men educated from a handful of universities maintained their hold on Indian nationalism. They rallied around Gandhi and effectively did not let Gandhi's appeal toward masses get translated into an egalitarian takeover of Indian nationalism and the freedom struggle it spawned. So, as Aligarh was the epicenter of Muslim Indian nationalism, it was the Presidency College in Calcutta, Elphinstone College in Bombay, and the universities of Calcutta, Bombay, Madras, and Allahabad that bred the men who dominated Indian nationalism in the vehicles of the Congress party or for that matter in parties such as the CPI. Higher education and politics in colonial India were intimately bound, and the university world played a key role in how Pakistani nationalism and Indian nationalism evolved in British colonial India.

Contrasting Nationalisms in the Educational Space

However, between the dominant political cultures of Muslim Indian nationalism and Indian nationalism, there were voices in education that, on the one hand, questioned the colonialist/nationalist educational ideal and, on the other hand, tried to explore philosophical universes beyond the narrow politics and oppressive political domination of nationalism. Rabindranath Tagore, India's national poet, had conceived and created a school and a university in Santiniketan, some 150 km away from Calcutta. His was an attempt to create an education that moved away from the colonial framework and embraced a new universalism. The Jamia Millia Islamia created by students and teachers dissatisfied with the functioning of AMU too was based on a critique of colonial education. Tagore actively took part in the anti-British *Swadeshi* (*swadesh* means "one's own land") movement in Bengal in 1905 but within some years, he became disillusioned with nationalism and nationalist politics.

He became a harsh critic of nationalism, and his 1917 book *Nationalism* admonished the Western world and Japan for their nationalisms, which he felt could only breed aggression. Ashis Nandy (1994) has discussed in detail the poet's critique of Indian nationalism, which can lead us to question the legitimacy of nationalism. Tagore is India's national poet, and yet his view on nationalism sits uncomfortably with the trumpeting of nationalism in pre- and post-independent India. Within the realm of the university, this discomfort has a history of faint murmurs. Partha Chatterjee (2016) recalls his encounter with Tagore's lectures on nationalism in a course on political thought at the University of Calcutta in the 1960s. Clearly, as Chatterjee himself notes, the professors in the university who exposed students to Tagore's passionate critique of nationalism were advancing a complex relationship between the university and nationalism. This critique of nationalism has continued as a thought current in the Indian university world. Before India's independence from colonial rule, at least two institutions epitomized this thought current; they were Jamia Millia Islamia and Tagore's Santiniketan school and Viswa Bharati.

I first turn to Jamia. Aligarh, that is, AMU, was founded with the declared aims of creating educated Muslim subjects of colonial rule, and though Aligarh became the nerve center of the Pakistan movement, the university's core educational paradigm remained bound to colonial patterns of education. The Urdu poet Akbar Illahabadi wrote about Aligarh's educational achievement with a heavy dose of irony:

> What glorious deeds our fellows have performed!
>
> Passed B.A., got a government job, received a pension and died. (Hasan 1998a: 157)

Along with the fixation for a job in the colonial bureaucracy, there was also the veneration of things English; there was a sense that if one could approximate to English/British cultural patterns, one became a truly civilized person. Muhammad Talib (1998) gives us a picture of the creation and development of Jamia. The institution was founded in October 1920, and the Old Boys' Lodge in Aligarh was its first home. After inhabiting several modest homes in the AMU neighborhood, Jamia moved to Delhi. In contrast to AMU's British colonial moorings and espousal of English-medium education, the founders of Jamia strongly advocated education through mother tongue; in Jamia's case, it was Urdu. Jamia's founders were determined to keep education free of British control, and the curriculum was planned such that it could be true to the religious and cultural traditions and upheld a morally guided path. Early 1920s was the time of the first pan-Indian movement against colonial rule; under Gandhi's leadership, the non-cooperation movement spread to all corners of British India and brought in great numbers of people into politics and anti-colonial struggle. Gandhi and his compatriots like the Ali brothers also led the Khilafat movement where they tried to pressure the British government to preserve the authority of the Ottoman emperor as the Caliph (Khalifa) of Islam whose power was greatly diminished at the end of the First World War in 1918. Khilafat and non-cooperation were the political moments at the birth of Jamia, and the institution was intimately linked to the political awakening of the time. Nationalism and anti-colonialism along with embracing of Islam formed the philosophical basis of education in the minds of the founders of Jamia. As much as it was born out of a critique of colonial education, it also distanced itself from the orthodox Muslim education imparted in madrasas.[7] The hallmark of Jamia's education was not its adoption of Urdu alone. More importantly, it founded an education which brought the aspiration for a purer existence through religion and the need for a real-life practical existence under the same roof. Jamia's students discussed the Quran and the Hadith, and at the same time, the curriculum focused on skills training in different trades such as agriculture, gardening, cooking, tailoring, weaving, and book-binding. Religion, nationalism, critical enquiry, and an embrace of the world of work and labor formed the bedrock of Jamia's educational universe. Much of these were to later inform Gandhi's educational thrust as seen in Buniyadi talim, in which Zakir Hussain, Jamia's leading thinker for a long time, was his closest comrade. In contrast to AMU, which emulated the colonial educational universe, Jamia Millia Islamia broke new ground in education. It questioned the colonial worldview and started a journey that brought anti-colonialism, national aspirations, Islam, and a respect for labor and culture of work into the rubric of education. While AMU fuelled the Pakistan movement and supplied the new Pakistani state with a section of the new elite, Jamia contributed to the fabric of a polyphonic India after 1947. AMU whose founding was centered on veneration of English/Western education contributed greatly to the state of Pakistan fashioned as a nation of India's Muslims, and Jamia founded with Islam as one of its pillars informed the plurality of India after 1947. In their two trajectories, we see a contrast in nationalisms. The eastern Oxford of Sir Syed's dream created a Muslim nation-state and Jamia with an adherence to Islam's role in education contributed to a multi-religious India.

Different Religio-cultural Worlds, Similar Educational Universes

Jamia was born in an Islamic fold. Viswa Bharati was born in a *Brahmo* fold. Yet, in their core values, the institutions had much in common. Their educational philosophy was against the colonial pattern of rote learning and manufacturing clerks to man the British Indian bureaucracy. Founding men of both institutions wanted education to be based on the spirit of free enquiry; they upheld universal goals and at the same time wanted to be true to religious and cultural traditions. And, in a distinct departure from Brahminical–colonial patterns, their idea of education was to link it intimately with the native soil where the institutions were located and to enmesh education with labor, laboring people and trades of ordinary everyday life.

While Jamia believed in Islam's creative role in the educational universe, Santiniketan and Viswa Bharati were born within the fold of the *Brahmo* movement. In the Europe–India encounter of nineteenth century, various cultural streams of Indian life underwent reform and new forms emerged. In Bengal with Calcutta as the epicenter, the *Brahmo* sect became prominent. The *Brahmo*s believed in single godhead and abhorred the idol worship prevalent in the traditional Hindu world. Drawing its following from wealthy upper-caste Hindu families, the *Brahmo*s contributed a great deal to the educational, cultural, and political development of Bengal and India. The *Brahmo* leader Rammohan Roy's campaign against Sati—the practice of burning a widow on the funeral pyre of her husband, contributed to the ban on Sati.

Rabindranath Tagore grew up in the *Brahmo* world of Calcutta. His poetry was deeply influenced by *Brahmo* ideas and ideals of divinity. As a teenager, Tagore was not at ease with the colonial education imparted in Calcutta schools of nineteenth century. In one of his short stories, he ridiculed the system of education which turned students into parrots.[1] In the *Brahmo* school he founded in Santiniketan, he wanted to impart an education that would be free from the oppressiveness of colonial education. The school was founded in 1901.[8] Freedom was central to Tagore's vision for the school. He wanted to unshackle Indians from the baggage of colonialism, but colonialism was not the only source of unfreedom. Brahminical and patriarchal worldviews also clouded Indian minds, and Tagore's school encountered those blocks on the path to educational freedom.

From the autobiography of a student in the early years of the school, quoted in a recent study (Ghosh and Sarkar 2015), we get to know that students belonging to different castes wore dresses of different colors; each color would be assigned to specific castes like Brahmins, Vaidyas, and Vaishyas.[9] In the dining hall, there were separate sitting arrangements for Brahmin and non-Brahmin students. In the early years of the school, in the case of non-Brahmin teachers, Brahmin students refused to bow down and touch their feet—a gesture of respect for elders; they would only do *namaskar* with folded hands. The educational climate was so ill-disposed toward the lower castes that a non-upper-caste teacher called Kunjalal was removed from teaching and assigned to administrative job.

With the resistance toward lower castes, one can guess that the community also would not accept Muslims with open arms. In 1910, a Muslim gentleman had wanted to send his son to the Santiniketan school but in spite of Tagore's insistence, the authorities of the ashram and the school did not give admission to the boy. In 1919, a Muslim boy from South Africa was enrolled for a short while. The school had to wait till December 1919 when a Bengali Muslim boy became the first full-time student of Santiniketan; this boy was called Syed Mujtaba Ali who went on to become a celebrated Bengali writer.

Girls too did not have an easy ride. In 1908, a girls' hostel came up but it had to be shut down in 1910. The principal reason was that the free mixing of boys and girls—which always creates tensions and excitement around the emotional exchanges of the two sexes—did not go down well with the authorities. Tagore expressed his sadness at this decision but he did not try to veto the decision of the school authorities. Girls had to wait till 1918 to become full-fledged members of the educational world of Santiniketan.

It is interesting to note the differences in social realities of Jamia and Santiniketan. Jamia emerged from within the Muslim universe and had very little, if at all, of caste distinction between students, at least there was no theoretical endorsement of caste in Islam. Second, born in the interstices of Islam and India's freedom movement under the leadership of Gandhi, non-Muslims or Hindus were much more welcome in Jamia from the very beginning. In fact that Jamia did not toe the Pakistan line that dominated Aligarh in late 1930s and 1940s itself is a pointer to its rejection of narrowly defined nationalism. However, while Santiniketan grappled with all the issues of caste, religion, and gender, Jamia did not open its doors to women students till much later in the day. That girls came back to the institution, Muslim students grew in number, and that in 1920, Brahmins and other castes started eating together in Santiniketan; all of this was in a large measure the influence of Gandhi and of the social change that accompanied the freedom movement. On the one hand, he visited the ashram a few times, once in 1915 and later in 1920, and more so because of the anti-British struggle he had launched across India. The freedom movement united Indians against an alien rule; it also broke down many walls that Indians had erected between one another for centuries. The history of Santiniketan in a microcosm captures the impulses of an India undergoing radical social change.

The school in Santiniketan was founded in 1901, and in 1918, the year that the First World War ended, Tagore initiated the process of creating a higher education institution. He called it Viswa Bharati (*Viswa* meaning world and Bharati defining *Bharat* that is India). And true to its name, the world came to Santiniketan. Tagore had won the Nobel Prize for literature in 1913, and writers, artists, intellectuals, and statesmen from home and the world came to see his educational universe. Some like C.F. Andrews and Leonard Elmhirst became key figures in the growth of that universe. But Tagore did not only open up Viswa Bharati to the knowledge universes of China, Japan, Europe, or the Arab world; he also insisted that students must observe the death anniversary of religious leaders such as Buddha, Christ, Muhammad, Chaitanya, Nanak, Kabir, and Rammohan. Along with respect for human thought, he also stressed on deep respect and interaction with nature. Tagore's educational vision in his school and later in Viswa Bharati was to create independent man, not the subjugated colonial subject. His lifelong mission was to unshackle the colonized mind.

But within the first two decades of the Santiniketan school, he could sense that the dreary world of routine was creeping its way into the school. He also observed the arrogance of the educated. His educational vision moved a step forward. In 1923, he started Siksha satra (Siksha meaning education), a school where the separation between work and knowledge would be done away with. This was also part of his vision of injecting Indian village life with new vigor. When Indians were immersed in rote learning and bookish education, he had sent his son and another student to learn agriculture in a university in America. While Jamia stressed on learning some trades, Siksha satra developed courses on a large variety of trades. House building, sanitation, cooking, public health, hospitality, making textile items, making paper, dyeing, making bricks, repairing cycles, and making musical instruments were some of them. When Gandhi visited Siksha satra in 1925, he was overwhelmed; he could see his vision of Buniyadi talim in Tagore's school. He even wanted to take a leading figure of Siksha satra to his Wardha ashram. Both Jamia and Santiniketan school/Siksha satra were deeply touched by the thrusts of Gandhi and the freedom movement. Both tried to free education from the oppressiveness of colonial educational system and at the same time steer clear of aggressive nationalisms, be it Muslim Indian nationalism or Indian nationalism. The two institutions tried to define education as a system of combining the world of work and the world of knowledge. But these impulses of educational freedom and universalism lost out to the votaries of aggressive nationalism. The votaries of aggressive nationalism won the day with one another's Pakistan and India. The university in Aligarh got its Pakistan; Presidency, Calcutta, Bombay, and Madras universities got their India; and the colonial education system largely continued in both nation-states.[10] Thrusts emanating from Jamia and Viswa Bharati toward non-Eurocentric universalism and toward combining the world of work and knowledge or giving primacy to village reconstruction remained a faint murmur. With Tagore's death in 1941 and Gandhi's murder in 1948, the possibilities of an education that would unshackle the colonized mind died soon thereafter.

Notes

1. For a history of the Hindu College/Presidency College, see Zachariah et al. (1998).
2. Among others, M. Rajivlochan (2008) has discussed how the London University served as the model for setting up the first universities in India. That model has largely dominated the pattern of Indian universities in the colonial and post-colonial eras.
3. I fashion this phrase on the lines of Samuel Huntington's phrase "clash of civilizations."

4. Books that document and analyze India's freedom movement are countless. Sumit Sarkar (1984) gives a balanced account of the freedom movement from the second half of nineteenth century till independence in 1947.
5. For an account of "national education," see University Education Commission (1950).
6. Self-sufficient village republics was the Gandhian ideal. However, one should be alert to the fact that historically we do not experience self-sufficient village republics in India. In Gandhi's worldview and scheme of things, there is a trend of idolizing the Indian village. I am aware that the Indian village is not a paradise, yet it is important to give adequate importance to rejuvenate village life economically as well as culturally and educationally. Rabindranath Tagore could see that the Indian village was in a state of decay, and his work in eastern Bengal in the first decade of twentieth century and in Santiniketan and Sriniketan in the first half of twentieth century was to rejuvenate rural Bengal. And Gandhi himself put social reform at the center even as he gave primacy to the Indian village in his conception of development.
7. Abdur Rahman Sehwarvi (Bijnori), an Aligarh graduate, outlined a proposal of the university, and while asserting that Urdu should be the medium of instruction, he also clarified that it did not mean a backward movement toward madrasa education. See Talib (1998).
8. The educational institutions that Rabindranath Tagore founded were at least three: First was a school in Santiniketan, the second was a center for higher learning which he named Viswa Bharati, and the third was Siksha satra, also a school but one where the learning of trades was put as part of the core curriculum. Siksha satra was also part of Sriniketan which was an institution he set up for the rejuvenation of Indian rural life and material condition. There are a number of studies on these institutions. See Dasgupta (1998), and Ghosh and Sarkar (2015). For an understanding of Tagore's educational thought, see Dasgupta (2009).
9. Ghosh and Sarkar (2015) quote from the autobiography of Rebachand, one of the first residents in the fully residential school in Santiniketan. According to Rebachand, each day after bath, students wore dresses; the Brahmin boy wore white silk, the Vaidya boy wore red silk, and the Vaishya boy wore yellow silk. In the caste patterns in Bengal, Vaidya is a caste between the Brahmin (priest) and Kshatriya (warrior), and here again unlike the north Indian caste structure, in Bengal, the Kshatriya caste is replaced by a caste called Kayastha.
10. From Commission on National Education (1959), formed by Ayub Khan's government in Pakistan, we learn that two American educationists were members; this was both a continuation of colonial influence and of

the post-1945 Cold War era politics, Pakistan being a close US ally in the Cold War period. Though Pakistan and India were divided on religious lines, the epistemological universe of the ruling elites of both nations was influenced by the Anglo-American world. There was no representation from Muslim societies outside the sub-continent in the making of post-independence educational policy of Pakistan, though Pakistan claimed itself to be the homeland of Indian Muslims.

Recommended Readings

Bhattachrya, Sabyasachi. (ed). 1998. *The Contested Terrain: Perspectives on Education in India.* New Delhi: Orient Longman.

Chatterjee, Partha. 2016. Freedom of Speech in the University. *Economic and Political Weekly* 51 (11): 35–37.

Commission on National Education. 1959. *Report of the Commission on National Education.* Islamabad: Government of Pakistan.

Dasgupta, Uma. 1998. *Santiniketan: The School of a Poet.* In Hasan 1998a.

Dasgupta, Uma (ed.). 2009. *The Oxford India Tagore: Selected Writings on Education and Nationalism.* New Delhi: Oxford University Press.

Ghosh, Swati, and Ashok Sarkar. 2015. *Kabir pathshala: pathabhavan o sikshasatrer itihas.* Calcutta: Signet Press.

Hasan, Mushirul. (ed.). 1998a. *Knowledge, Power & Politics: Educational Institutions in India.* New Delhi: Roli Books.

Hasan, Mushirul. 1998b. *Negotiating with Its Past and Present: The Changing Profile of the Aligarh Muslim University.* In Hasan 1998a.

Kumar, Deepak. 1998. Educational Ideas of Bengali Scientists from 1850 to 1920. In Bhattacharya.

Kumar, Krishna. 1991. *Political Agenda of Education—A Study of Colonialist and Nationalist Ideals.* New Delhi: Sage.

Nandy, Ashis. 1994. The Illegitimacy of Nationalism—Rabindranath Tagore and the Politics of Self. New Delhi: Oxford University Press.

Rajivlochan, M. 2008. Reforming Education for India, from England. *Seminar* 587: 39–42.

Sarkar, Sumit. 1984. *Modern India 1885–1947.* New Delhi: Macmillan.

Talib, Mohammad. 1998. Jamia Millia Islamia: Career of Azad Talim. In Hasan 1998a.

University Education Commission. 1950. *Report of the University Education Commission (UEC).* New Delhi: Government of India.

Zachariah, B., S.R. Chakraborti, and R.K. Ray. 1998. Presidency College, Calcutta: An Unfinished History. In Hasan 1998a.

CHAPTER 4

Cold War to Brand Wars: Global Processes, Developmental Visions, and Indian Higher Education

Abstract "Cold War to Brand Wars" discusses global processes, developmental visions, and Indian higher education. Modern and contemporary India's development and ideas of development are inextricably linked to the policies set in motion during British colonial rule. Indian elites' conception of development was heavily influenced by their exposure to development in Britain and in Western Europe. The pattern of the Indian mind to fashion development along Western lines took a new step forward with independence. Post-1947 India was faced with a bipolar world of superpower rivalry between the USA and the USSR. The Cold War impacted India's development, its higher education, and the policy environment. The decades since 1990 have seen the impact of globalization and a new era of world politics. This chapter discusses the impact of global processes on Indian development and higher education policy and narrates the shifts in India's developmental visions. The selective use of science by Indian policy planners, a specific view of the West within dominant Indian opinion and a particular understanding of development, has impacted India's policy in higher education. The author argues that a narrow and elite-serving view of development has had limiting impact on the growth and flowering of Indian higher education and society.

Keywords Commanding heights of economy
Commanding heights of education · Science as liberator
Brands and branding · India/Bharat divide · Educational democracy

S. Roy Chowdhury, *Politics, Policy and Higher Education in India*,
DOI 10.1007/978-981-10-5056-5_4

End of Colonialism, Beginning of Cold War

In 1947, at the time of India's independence, the world order that colonized India knew was experiencing profound changes. For India, there were three changes. The first was independence. In its newfound independence, India could surely plan to chart its own course in economy, developmental agenda, education, and areas of national interest. The second was that the Western imperial powers of eighteenth and nineteenth centuries; most notably, Britain and France were gradually losing control of their colonial territories and, among the Western nations, the United States of America (USA) was increasingly taking the lead in global affairs and was the new leader of the "free world." The third change was the rise of the Soviet Union. The Russian Revolution of 1917 had ushered in the Soviet Union (USSR), and after a victorious role in the Second World War (1939–1945), it became a great power in world politics. It also symbolized communism as opposed to the capitalism of America, Britain, France, and other Western nations. America and the Soviet Union became the leaders of the capitalist and socialist camps, respectively, which led to the beginning of Cold War that lasted from the late 1940s until the end of the Soviet Union in 1991. India had a profound change at home; it had become an independent nation. And, in the world, it did not have to engage with the might of Britain, but the new world leaders were the capitalist USA and the socialist Soviet Union. America was the new great power and leader among the rich Western nations. And, on the world stage, it was no longer a singular domination of capitalist West but a socialist Soviet Russia had become an equal politico-military power.

This change in global structure impacted political, economic, and educational thought in post-1947 India. In the decades preceding independence, India had experienced a robust anti-colonial struggle and the flowering of ideas and ideals under the leadership of Gandhi and Gandhian thought. For independent India, the charm and influence of the Gandhian ideal were greatest. Education was one of the centerpieces in Gandhi's thought universe. In South Africa and later in India, he led a life that was meant to be a model for others to get educated in his path and follow it. As he famously said, "My life is my teaching." Gandhi's political ideal lay in the non-violent overthrow of the British Raj while his economic ideal lay in the rejuvenation of India's village life. In sync with his economic ideal, rural life and its rejuvenation were central to the educational universe of Gandhi. Even as Gandhi waged his struggle against colonialism, a large part of the Indian upper and middle classes were under the spell of English and Western civilization. They did side with Gandhi on the question of political independence and control of the state mechanism, but their philosophical world, culturally and materially, was heavily influenced by Britain. Alongside English, science constituted a vital part of the appeal of Western civilization for the educated and affluent Indian. The dominant belief in the superiority of English as a language and in the power of science to transform India's economy was profoundly etched in the minds of most educated Indians.[1] Gandhi had challenged this worldview but he had limited success. At independence, while the Gandhian way was one of the paths of development before the new nation, the elite was inherently inclined in adopting Western modes of economic progress. However, with the rise of socialism and the Soviet Union, the options of development paths did not remain only one "Western way." Alongside the capitalist path, a new choice emerged on the horizon; that of socialism, especially in the reality of Soviet Union.

Of Gandhi, Tagore, and Rural University

The elite could now sidestep the Western Anglo-American domination and choose to benefit from the power and knowledge base of Soviet Union. The precise influence of Soviet Russia on India's educational thought can be discerned in policy documents such as the EC of 1964–1966. The more important question is the developmental vision of independent India's political, economic, and educational elite. Indian higher education had developed in the 150-year colonial period, principally, in the shadow of British structures of higher education. Scholars like M. Rajivlochan (2008) have demonstrated how the first Indian universities were built on the London university model. With anti-colonial movement and upsurge in nationalist ideas and ideals, and with the overarching influence of Gandhi and of men like Tagore, Indian political opinion challenged British rule, and finally, colonial rule came to an end. During the anti-colonial struggle, small groups of educated and vocal Indians started alternative economic activities such as during the Swadeshi movement in Bengal in 1905–1907 or the different voluntary organizations Gandhi founded and led. Gandhi and his followers developed a worldview that posited itself against colonial domination and Western modernity. Tagore's work in Santiniketan, Sriniketan, and

Siksha Satra was also an Indian answer to colonial domination of Indian education.[2] But the appeal of this alternative universe started fading soon after independence. The alternative philosophical thrust of Gandhi and Tagore did not get woven into the specific path of industrial development that post-1947 India charted for itself. In its developmental vision, independent India continued with the fetish of English language and modern science. This, in turn, shaped the dominant Indian thinking on higher education.

In the initial years after independence, UEC of 1948–1949 reflects the developmental vision of Gandhi. The commission was formed by Government of India; it had ten members with Sarvepalli Radhakrishnan, who later became the second president of India, as its chairman. Three of the ten members were foreign nationals: one from the UK and two from America. This choice reflected three strands. First, Indian anti-colonial struggle led by Gandhi was against British political domination but it had a declared policy that it was not against the Western world. Second, among the world powers, it was America who unequivocally supported India's right to independence. Third, and probably the most significant politically, this choice also represented India's perception and acceptance of America as the dominant world power in politics, economy, and education.

While the influence of world politics can be discerned, the mark of Gandhian thought and a larger humanistic worldview can also be observed. The chairman of the commission was Sarvepalli Radhakrishnan, a philosopher who in his erudition synthesizes Western and Eastern philosophical traditions. The awe of science and technology had not yet completely mesmerized the national elite. And, though there were more Americans than British in the commission, one of the Americans was an educator with deep-rooted experience in working with rural education issues in America. This reflects the influence of Gandhi.

UEC puts forward a vision of education and development where rural India had a central place. While this vision is praiseworthy, at the same time, it disappoints us with the conservative view on women and public life. It argued that "the best place" for women was in the homes, and based on this patriarchal view, the commission conceived women's participation in education. This resulted in the neglect of women within the framework of higher education thinking and policymaking.

The developmental vision centered on Gandhian swaraj, and the rural world is of relevance even today. Its neglect by subsequent policymaking has diminished the social transformative roles of Indian higher education. UEC laid great stress on rural universities and on agricultural education. The commission's period coincided with the time when the Indian Constitution was being shaped in the Constituent Assembly of free India. The spirit of freedom movement and the Constitution informed UEC:

> The outlines of the social philosophy which should govern all our institutions, educational as well as economic and political, are indicated in the preamble of our Draft Constitution. We are engaged in a quest for democracy through the realization of justice, liberty, equality and fraternity. We shall take up the different problems of educational theory and practice and arrange them under the five heads of democracy, justice, liberty, equality and fraternity.

World political processes such as the French Revolution of 1789 inform the policy document; the clarion call of the revolution, "liberty, equality, fraternity," is upheld by the policymakers. While the social justice content of India's freedom struggle and the spirit of Constitution inform the UEC, one can also discern the influence of world communism. They refer to Karl Marx's thought, saying:

> The education of the future will in the case of every child over a certain age, combine productive labor with education and athletics not merely as one of the methods of raising social production but as the only method of producing fully developed human beings. On this question of learning through doing Marx and Gandhi agree.

Here, we discern how the authors are marrying the influence of global socialist ideals, whose influence on the Indian thought world of 1930s and 1940s was enormous, and the thought world of Gandhi.[3] For conceptualizing and advocacy of integrating physical and manual labor in the educational process, they draw inspiration from two thinkers who have often been seen as providing succor to two distinct political streams in modern and contemporary India.[4] While discussing justice, UEC argues a democratic society "... must raise the material standards of life and increase national productivity by the larger use of scientific discoveries and technical application."

They point to Soviet Russia as to how the socialist state

> wiped out illiteracy, raised the educational level of the masses, built and equipped scientific institutes and laboratories and transformed the country with new industries and new type of agriculture.

Significantly, UEC shows appreciation of “new industries” and “new types of agriculture” in the Soviet Union. This new industry was state-controlled industry, and this new agriculture was collective farming. The policy thinkers hold in high esteem the principles of command economy as was practiced in the erstwhile Soviet Union. Here, we see a two-pronged discourse: On the one hand, there was the appeal of communist ideology as spelt out in Marx’s thought; on the other hand, there was the appeal of state-led and state-commanded economic growth model of the real-life socialist system developed in the Soviet Union.

While I point out the influences of global ideational and political processes on the thought pattern of the commission, this in no way reduces the significance of UEC’s recommendations. Three areas which the commission stresses upon in order to advance the cause of justice, namely, agricultural education, technological education, and rural development, remain as important as ever. Cottage industries assume an important role within rural development:

> cottage industries and small cooperatives require to be developed and machines to lighten the labours of men living in cottages.

In the developmental vision of UEC, agricultural and technical education and rural development are intertwined; later and contemporary educational policy moved away substantially from their vision where the village had a central role in policy imagination.

Religious education forms another important strand of thinking in UEC. No other policy document in independent India has put forward the case of religious education, not to mention the thrust that UEC gave it. The overarching concern of Radhakrishnan and his colleagues was the preservation and continuity of the pluralist world of India; they wanted students to be exposed to multiple belief systems. Their stress on religious education came in the aftermath of the partition of British India, which was accompanied before and after, by ghastly riots between Hindus, Muslims, and Sikhs; millions were uprooted from their generations-old homes.

While some policy thinkers had previously advocated that religious education was best left to families, UEC differed[5]:

> If we are not prepared to leave the scientific and literary training of pupils to the home and the community, we cannot leave religious training to these. ... The child is robbed of its full development. ... If this guidance is left to homes and communities, the chances are that communal bigotry, intolerance and selfishness may increase.

Taking note of the secular state in India, the UEC recommended:

> that all educational institutions start work with a few minutes for silent meditation, that in the first year of the degree course lives of the great religious leaders like Gautama the Buddha, Confucius, Zoroaster, Socrates, Jesus, Samkara, Ramanuja, Madhava, Mohammed, Kabir, Nanak, Gandhi, be taught; that in the second year some selections of a universalist character from the Scriptures of the world be studied, and that in the third year, the central problem of philosophy of religion be considered.

Their recommendation reflects the influence of Gandhi and other thinkers of peace such as Tagore, who emerged during the freedom struggle. They also find ways to address the scar of partition where religious passion inflamed millions of people and led to nothing but destruction and misery. An urge for peace in education must have also informed the authors of the report, especially after the horrors of the Second World War, no less that the war ended with America's atom-bombing of the Japanese cities of Hiroshima and Nagasaki.[6] The practice of exposing undergraduate students in various disciplines to religious and thought leaders from diverse cultures of the world would have not only made them more understanding and accepting of one another's religious beliefs but also would have created a wider world consciousness in them. In the last 70 years, dominant public world and policy thinking in India has moved away from the pluralist-humanitarian thought of UEC; a new developmental vision has gradually engulfed the nation.

Commanding Heights of Economy, Education, and Science

The Gandhian developmental vision was replaced quickly in the early years of independent India with an economic vision where science, technology, and management became the core of developmental thought. Along with advisers like the scientists P.C. Mahalanobis, Vikram Sarabhai and Meghnad Saha, and the industrialist J.N. Tata, Prime Minister Nehru led India to a specific path of economic and industrial development, where high science, mega developmental projects, and new industrial townships became the central design of Indian developmental planning. The idea of economic growth with rural India at its center was relegated to the backseat. Science as a panacea of most of India's ills became the new mantra of development.[7] With big dams and mega steel plants encapsulating Nehru's concept of "commanding heights of economy," Indian agriculture too underwent profound changes.[8] The Green Revolution in Punjab, Haryana, and western Uttar Pradesh raised agricultural productivity manifold, but has also left behind environmental and agricultural problems. This developmental vision which was completely top-down attitude developed from the core idea of science in command and gave shape to the three strands of commanding heights of economy, science and technology, and education.

While the founding of the Indian Institutes of Technology (IITs) and the Indian Institutes of Management (IIMs) had already initiated the structure of commanding heights of education, EC (1964–1966) which worked close on the heels of Nehru's death in 1964 embodied the dominant developmental ideology of India of 1950s and 1960s. It also reflected acutely the influence of Cold War and of Soviet Union on Indian thought world. The selection of the head of the commission is itself an important pointer to the change of ideas and ideals. While the philosopher Radhakrishnan led UEC in 1948–1949, in 1964–1966, the governing elite thought D.S.Kothari, a professor of physics to be best suited for the job of chairing the commission. EC was a mammoth exercise, and its four-volume report remains the most comprehensive survey of Indian education. Several recommendations were definitely well thought and apt; however, EC was clearly part of a thought structure where the commanding heights of education fed into the "commanding heights of economy." A humanist educational and socio-economic vision was replaced by a bureaucratic and techno-scientific vision, and EC bore that imprint.

UEC's vision of creating rural universities disappears from the idea world of EC. While the importance of agricultural universities remains, EC stresses upon creation of major universities and metropolitan universities:

> The most important reform we envisage is the development of five or six what we may call major universities where conditions may be provided ... to make first-class post-graduate work and research work possible.

Clearly, a vision and policy of creating elite centers of higher education informs the idea of major universities. When the commission advocates "*conditions may be provided ... to make first-class post-graduate work and research work possible,*" what is evident is that high-class education and research will not happen in the non-major universities. That is a clear indication that while most universities will remain financially and educationally poor, the policy decision is to create a handful of elite centers of higher education. Soon after EC, we see the founding of JNU in Delhi, which becomes an elite center of higher education, especially in the social sciences. The idea of setting up metropolitan universities in the major cities of India also finds favor with the urban-centric Indian planning process. In the decades since 1970, we have seen an increasing concentration of universities in the big Indian cities. In a way, the major university and the metropolitan university ideas have coalesced. There is no major university under the aegis of the government, apart from the setting up of IITs or IIMs, which has been planned or has developed in a small Indian town, not to mention rural India.

EC discusses the national preoccupation with science and technology and underscores the need of social sciences and humanities. However, this discussion does not lead EC or the planning processes it impacted to give a strong fillip to the growth of humanities and social sciences at the undergraduate or postgraduate levels. A handful of elite social science research centers developed under the aegis of Indian Council of Social Science Research (ICSSR). Though EC talks about the national preoccupation of science and technology, its own vision is also under the hegemony of science and technology. In its reference to global contexts, it says:

> … the greatest contribution of Europe doubtlessly is the scientific revolution.

The same thought world informs the stress on Russian as a preferred language. EC advocated that for anyone wanting to get a Ph.D. degree, she/he must learn Russian; it even suggested that the government should consider whether or not to make Russian compulsory at the master's level. This affinity toward learning Russian was definitely not for love of Tolstoy, Dostoyevsky, or Russian literature. The scientific and technological prowess of the Soviet Union, that it could create mega industries and could send man into space or that it could create a nuclear arsenal, is what caught the imagination of Indian educationists. So, policy thinking was informed by the politics of Cold War and a global political situation where India's foreign policy tilted gradually toward the Soviet Union and a staunch belief system that the techno-scientific path was the only way for development. The techno-scientific vision was accompanied by an urban and elite-centric growth path. One fed into the other. The impact of global processes, a vision of techno-scientific development and an elite-centric politics, informed and shaped policy-making of EC and the India of late 1960s and 1970s. The commanding heights of economy that were much appreciated by Prime Minister Nehru found its perfect match in the commanding heights of education as they emerged from EC's discourse and policy advocacy.

Though EC abandons the idea of rural university, agricultural universities, vocational education, and education for women get high priority. Discussing agricultural universities, EC recommended that alongside traditional subject areas like plant pathology or soil science, academic courses should be developed in fields such as engineering for agriculture, food technology, agricultural economics, public administration, mass communication, sociology, anthropology, law, earth sciences, basic sciences, and humanities. EC saw agricultural education much beyond agriculture alone. The agricultural university that they envisioned was a university with the widest possible interest in knowledge disciplines, which had a special focus on agricultural education. Going further, they proposed setting up of agricultural colleges and agricultural polytechnics, and recommended that agricultural education be included in the syllabus of secondary schools. Apart from one recommendation to bring agriculture into the public space, that of broadcasting agricultural programs through radio, nearly all the valuable recommendations concerning agricultural education found few takers.[9] The reality of agricultural university and agricultural education did not live up to their vision. Agriculture with an annual growth rate of 3% or less remains one of the worst performing sectors of Indian economy. "Shining India" seldom thinks that the number of malnourished and undernourished children is about a quarter of the population, and even for the large low and middle middle-classes, the intake of fruits and vegetables is limited to a very small variety. The neglect of agriculture and agricultural education continues only at the peril of the nation's well-being.

EC stressed on vocational education as well. It says, it was unfortunate that there was a feeling "that vocational education at the school level is an inferior form of education, fit only for those who fail in general education, and the last choice of parents and students." The commission urges:

> A concerted effort is needed by both government and industry, through enlightened wage policies, vocational guidance and the education of public opinion, to promote the status and value of the skilled craftsman and technician. ... Our main recommendation is that, by 1986, some 20 per cent of all enrolments at the lower secondary level and some 50 per cent beyond class X should be in part-time or full-time vocational and professional courses.

Fifty years later, in 2017, neither do we see much of an enlightened wage policy nor has there been any uplift in the status and value of skilled craftsman. Pulls and pressures of the market economy may have led youth in the 18+ age group toward professional courses but educational planning has done scarce little to lead students after class X toward full-time vocational courses. The second United Progressive Alliance (UPA) government of 2009–2014 and the National Democratic Alliance (NDA) government of 2014–2019 have both discussed and promoted "Skill India," a new nomenclature for vocational education. But how far the change has happened at the ground level is uncertain. The skills of skilled workmen and workwomen remain unshaped by institutional education, and educational institutions do scarce little to change the skills gap in economy and society. Sadly enough, what is referred to as vocational education in India can never get a facelift unless the nation struggles against and overcomes the deep inequities of caste and class and the mentality of caste that plagues India.

Science as Commandment, Scientist as Oracle

While agricultural universities and vocational education were major areas of thrust in EC, the commission rested on the pillar of modern science. In their words:

> The basic approach and philosophy underlying the reconstruction of education adopted by us in this Report rests on our deep conviction that the progress, welfare and security of the nation depend critically on a rapid, planned and sustained growth in the quality and extent of education and research in science and technology. Science has radically transformed man's material environment. In the technologically advanced countries the average span of human life has increased more than a third over the last hundred years. Science is universal and so can be its benefits. Its material benefits are immense and far-reaching—industrialization of agriculture and release of nuclear energy, to mention two examples—but even more profound is its contribution to culture. Science is liberating and enriching of the mind and liberating of the human spirit. ... Nothing comparable to the scientific revolution in its impact on man's development and outlook has happened since the neolithic times.

We can hear a complete trust in science as the liberator of mankind. It is important to note the two examples of the benefits of science. Industrialization of agriculture as was envisaged and executed in northern and northwestern India in the 1960s along with the building of big dams and mega irrigation projects is one of the examples. The second example, nuclear power, civilian, and military, military even more than civilian, has fired the imagination of the power elite and the university-educated middle classes almost through the entire span of independent India. The specific pattern of science that is embraced is one which feeds into a power-centric celebration of national pride; the politics of nuclear power has fed into ultra-nationalist rhetoric often, especially in the late 1990s, when India under Prime Minister Vajpayee detonated the nuclear bomb.[10]

The placing of science at the high pedestal is also reflected in EC's advocacy of setting up of national science academy modeled on the lines of similar academies in Japan and the Soviet Union. Once again, the Soviet influence is strong on the policymakers. This belief in science as the liberator notwithstanding EC leaves behind a trail of ambivalence. While, on the one hand, science is seen as the great deliverer of development, on the other hand, that same hegemony is jolted when it quotes a scientist no less than Max Born:

> Though I love science I have the feeling that it is so much against history and tradition that it cannot be absorbed by our civilization. The political and military horrors and the complete breakdown of ethics which I have witnessed during my life may be not a symptom of an ephemeral social weakness but a necessary consequence of the rise of science—which in itself is one of the highest intellectual achievements of man. If this is so, there will be an end to man as free, responsible being. Should the race not be extinguished by a nuclear war it will degenerate into a flock of stupid, dumb creatures under the tyranny of dictators who will rule them with the help of machines and electronic computers.

Words like that leave the developmental vision of Nehruvian India and of EC with plenty of questions. The critique of a blind belief in science as the driver of development has developed in India and globally in recent times through the ideas of environmental activists, political psychologists, educationists, doctors, philosophers, and spiritual leaders. Much of that spirit had informed India through the works and writings of Gandhi and Tagore, which in turn was embodied in UEC (1948–1949). But India of 1960s and EC decided to bask in the sun called science. Later education policy too turned its back to the spirit of the philosophers.

Electorate and Education: No Longer an Elite Vision

In 1947, and especially with the adopting of the Constitution on January 26, 1950, India chose to be a parliamentary democracy with universal adult suffrage as a central pillar of its body politic. Four decades later, in the National Policy on Education (1986–1992), the voice of that body politic was loud and clear. The elite vision of EC gave way to a substantially more democratic vision of education. Soon after EC had submitted its report, the Congress which had been in power for two decades in almost all the Indian states was voted out of power in nine out of the sixteen states of that time. Though it strengthened itself with the Indian victory of the Indo-Pak war of 1971 and the creation of independent Bangladesh, it again lost popularity in 1975 when then prime minister Indira Gandhi, daughter of Jawaharlal Nehru, imposed Emergency and suspended all civic freedoms including the freedom of speech. A countrywide movement under the charismatic leadership of socialist Gandhian Jayaprakash Narayan united a great variety of opposition parties, and the amalgam called Janata Party came to power in Delhi in 1977, the first non-Congress government to rule India since independence in 1947. The Janata regime lasted barely 3 years. But it signaled significant changes in Indian political culture. Nehru or his daughter Indira was from the topmost echelons of the Indian elite; the coterie of their well-heeled advisers represented the bureaucratic/business/academic elite. In the Janata government, we see the appointment of Charan Singh, son of a Jat farmer from the state of Uttar Pradesh, as deputy prime minister and, briefly, even as prime minister. The power of the brown sahib, that is, the English-educated Westernized Indian elite, started to decline in the political sphere.

In 1980, the Congress stormed back to power in Delhi. While Congress reinforced itself as a central power, the nation was witness to violent struggles in different parts of the country. In the northwest, Sikh insurgents led by Jarnail Singh Bhindranwale wanted a separate nation-state for the Sikh people, and in Assam, the native Assamese people wanted to get rid of Bengalis and other "foreigners"—Indians who were resident in the state and flourished in business and other professions. In Andhra Pradesh, the Telugu Desam Party led by film-star turned politician N.T. Rama Rao stormed to power in the state elections, heralding the beginning of a strong current of state-centric and region-centric politics in India; a trend that championed greater decentralization of power. The Communist Party of India (Marxist) [CPI-M] was often in power in three states: two in the east and one in the south; they too continually attacked Indira Gandhi and the Congress for being unfair to the legitimate economic and other demands of the states. The 1980s can be seen in Indian politics as the decade of upsurge of regional parties, i.e., political parties whose electoral base is limited to a certain state of the country, and who represent the interests of people of a certain dominant linguistic/identity group concentrated in that particular state. In the 70s and 80s, the elite domination of politics gets challenged and New Delhi's unitary rule gets chipped away by the federal pulls of different Indian states. With Indira Gandhi's death through a brutal murder committed by her Sikh bodyguards, her son Rajiv Gandhi comes to power with a massive electoral victory in 1985. The new regime tries to respond to these two pressures, namely, against elitism and the centrist rule of New Delhi through a push to local self-governance; it gives a concerted push to the Panchayati Raj institutions, a system designed to create self-governance at the village level.[11] Rajiv does not return to power in the parliamentary elections of 1989; for a second time, a Janata-style government of an amalgam of parties and political ideologies spanning the right, the center, and the left come to power. The United Front government of Prime Minister V.P. Singh also lasts only 2 years, but once again, the push against elite domination is seen in his policies, especially in his extending reservations in education and government jobs to different backward castes/classes of the nation.

In the world arena too, there was a quiet change. The Soviet Union which was the great and only important light of the socialist/communist ideal in the 1950s gradually came to be challenged by communist China in the 1960s and 1970s. The leadership of world socialism/communism got divided into two rival camps. In the 1950s, beaming with confidence after successful freedom struggles against respective colonialisms, the leaders of new Asia and new Africa like India's Nehru, Indonesia's Suharto, Egypt's Gamal Abdel Nasser, and Ghana's Kwame Nkrumah, along with Josip Broz Tito of Yugoslavia, founded the Non-Aligned Movement (NAM), a bloc of nations who were non-aligned to and were equidistant from both the USA and the USSR. With the demise of the founding leaders, NAM slowly lost steam in 1970s, and by late 1980s, it had lost much of its substance. On the other hand, unable to reform itself and address certain emerging problems, the Soviet Union collapsed in 1991. While Nehru had maintained some sort of equal distance from America and Russia, Indira Gandhi leaned closer to the Soviet Union and created a range of arrangements that deepened Indo-Soviet political and economic ties in 1970s. With the end of the Soviet Union in 1991, India had suddenly lost its most important political and economic friend on the world stage. So, in the beginning of 1990s, both in domestic and international fronts, it was a substantially altered reality. The educational policymaking of this period reflects these profound changes that happened at home and in the world.

The National Policy on Education (NPE), initially enunciated in 1986, was further revised in 1991–1992; the recommendations of Ramamurti Committee (1990) and the work of a committee headed by Janardhana Reddy, then chief minister of Andhra Pradesh, were taken into consideration. The modified National Policy on Education was tabled to the parliament in 1992. It is best to designate this as NPE (1986–1992). NPE does not talk of building major universities; instead, the policy thinkers turn their attention to rural universities, and it introduces the idea of open universities in Indian educational planning. It gives a strong push toward women's education. Among its concerns is quality education for the physiologically challenged.

The center–state relation, i.e., the relationship between New Delhi and the different Indian states in the political sphere, impacts policy thinking in education. NPE is the first major policy document that categorically points to the structure that education was on concurrent list, meaning both the central government in Delhi and the state governments had purview over education. This implied that in the field of education, both were valid players and had important roles to play.

While the role of the states is given importance, NPE is once again the first policy document to lay a clear stress on women's education. In terms of political structures, it brings the states in as important players, and in the sphere of relationship between the two genders, it stresses the need for educational development of the deprived half of Indian society. Soon after 1947, UEC had decided that women's roles were mostly inside the house. NPE made a clear break from that patriarchal view of society; its thrust is clearly on women's education and women's empowerment through professional engagement. The introduction of women's studies departments in universities is recognition of academic discipline's role in addressing changing social and political reality. NPE signals a radical shift of policy in favor of women's empowerment. It also reflects the growing assertion of women and women's rights groups on the Indian policymaking process and in Indian polity.

The trajectory of women's empowerment went through a spurt during the freedom struggle in the first half of twentieth century, when a section of women from the affluent and educated classes came into public life. However, this spurt failed to impact policy in the immediate post-1947 years. In the 1950s and 1960s, the women's liberation movement became a strong presence in the West. This reinvigorated women's movement in India in the 1970s and 1980s, resulting in women's empowerment; its impact can be seen in later developments such as the creation of women's resource centers in undergraduate colleges and universities. Thrust on women's education in NPE is a symbol of the changed perceptions, so also is the discussion on education for the physiologically challenged. NPE is the first policy text that clearly advocates the case of better education for the disabled. A process of acceptance of the physiologically challenged in educational institutions may have started after NPE but its impact is still minimal. While major and metropolitan universities were the hallmark of EC, the flagship idea of NPE was open universities; it gave a strong push to open and distance education. This document stands out for its policy push for creating open universities that resulted in the growth of open universities since the early 1990s. While Indira Gandhi National Open University (IGNOU) set up by the central government has done phenomenal work in providing tertiary/higher education to millions of Indians young and old, state governments too have started their open universities. To an extent, this educational tool has revolutionized higher/tertiary education in India. Its inclusiveness has brought millions into the fold of higher education. What mobile telephony has done to communication, open learning systems have a similar potential in higher/tertiary education.

Open universities have had positive impacts in developing economies such as Thailand. The first open university was founded in 1970 in Thailand, a good two decades before India.[12] Compared to Thailand, India lags well behind its eastern neighbor in almost all the indicators of education, health, and economic well-being. Open learning systems and an appropriate language policy, I believe, have contributed a great deal to the success story of Thailand and many of India's South-East and East Asian neighbors.[13] Hence, the push of NPE (1986–1992) toward open and distance education makes it a landmark policy document in Indian education. When Rajiv Gandhi pushed forward the Panchayati Raj institutions, V.P. Singh implemented the Mandal Commission recommendations of extending educational and job reservations to the Other Backward Classes (OBCs); at the same juncture, NPE gave a strong push to open learning. Indian policymakers could feel that learning must move beyond the university walls; it was an urgent business to foster open learning systems in a democratic India.

Philosopher, Physicist, Politician, Private Industrialists

So far, I have shown how politics, both at the national and international levels, and education policy are interwoven. The trend continues in post-Cold War India. In the 1980s, President Ronald Reagan of the USA and Prime Minister Margaret Thatcher of the UK propagated less government intervention in the economy and greater privatization. This phenomenon came to be commonly referred to as Reaganomics. The World Bank and the International Monetary Fund (IMF) also advocated that greater trade between nations leads to greater prosperity. International trade in goods and services and movement of capital and labor got a great spurt in the decades following 1990–1991. The idea of less government in economic affairs of the nation and maximum role of private capitalists in nearly all sectors of life became the new mantra. In post-1991 India, this economic ideology, often referred to as liberalization, privatization, and globalization, came to be accepted across the political spectrum—left, right, and center.

This reliance on private industry and big corporations found expression in a post-1991 policy document. During NDA regime (1999–2004), in 2000, a special subject group within the Prime Minister's Council on Trade and Industry worked on and published a report called *A Policy Framework for Reforms in Education* (PFRE). Industrialists Mukesh Ambani and Kumar Mangalam Birla were, respectively, convenor and member of this group. It bears the hallmark of a new era of liberalization, privatization, and globalization. While a philosopher chaired UEC (1948–1949), a physicist led EC (1964–1966), and politicians had a leadership in NPE (1986–1992), in the new India with its mantra of private capital, two leading industrialists get appointed by the Prime Minister to create PFRE. The Indian power elite and the nation had journeyed a long way from Gandhi's swaraj to market raj.

The report looks at challenges in education and points out that education was important for economic growth. The authors of PFRE 2000 are acutely aware of the depths of poverty and troubles of governmental control and inefficient bureaucracy in India:

> The challenge that we face in education in India is to bridge the large gap between education have-nots and haves while, simultaneously, radically upgrading education content, delivery and processes to foster a competitive, yet cooperative, knowledge based society.

On the relation between education and development, PFRE points out:

> Education … is vital for population control, poverty reduction, economic growth, civic order, culture and citizenship. Education helps reduce poverty by increasing the productivity of the poor, reducing fertility rates, improving health and equipping people with the skills they need to participate fully in economy and society.

Linking the business and investment angle to education and development, it says:

> investment in education was considered more of a social obligation rather than one that would give significant returns.

They argue that the current understanding was that an educated population gave rise to higher economic indicators. They draw on the experience of South-East Asian nations and try to establish a correlation between greater economic input in education and their newfound prosperity. The report argues that human capital levels act as a driver of technological innovation and also determines the speed of absorption of technology.

Stressing upon the need to invest in education, PFRE finds that India has neglected investment in education. The discussion turns to NPE (1986–1992) which had advocated that expenditure on education should reach 6% of GDP. PFRE laments that the level of investment was nowhere near the 6% mark. And, on educational development in India, it sums up:

> India's education system is highly skewed. India has excellent examples of institutions at all levels of education to demonstrate its capability. Some higher education institutions like IITs and IIMs have earned international acclaim. But below this elite crust there is not much to speak of and the road ahead is challenging.

PFRE is aware of the social and economic challenges, about the depths of poverty and exclusion; it points out that schooling was still a costly proposition for the agricultural laborer and refers to the PROBE survey and states that sending two children to school amounts to nearly 40 days' wage for an agricultural laborer.[14] It also points out:

> We have rigid labor laws that protect the interests of 30 million employees in the government, public sector and organized private sector. The large numbers of workers in the unorganized sector and agriculture have no protection.

Rigidity, as PFRE rightly points out, does not stop with labor laws; it says education is a highly controlled sector and a plethora of rules and regulations act as a drag on the education system:

> Rules and regulations govern virtually everything from location, student intake, course content, fees and fee structure, appointments, compensation for faculty and so on ... Consequently institutions have become rigid. There is little freedom for creativity and innovation. The compensation system is unable to attract good quality faculty. Research initiatives are constrained and linkages with private sector are poor.

For the state of universities, PFRE also blames politicization; it states that Indian universities are hotbed of politics where teachers have turned into politicians and student unions are seen as nurseries of political careers. They urge political parties to come to an understanding and decide to stay away from universities and educational institutions.

PFRE suggests ways of improvement and change; it advocates foreign direct investment in higher education, and more importantly, it argues for decentralization of management of education:

> Redefinition of government role in higher education will call for a major privatization of the university education system in India. A Private University bill should be legislated to encourage establishment of new private universities in the fields of science and technology, management, economics, financial management and other critical areas with commercial application.

This report stands out for its advocacy of privatization of Indian higher education. Led by private capitalists, and coming in an era commonly referred to as a time of liberalization, privatization, and globalization, it initiates the idea of a private university bill. In the same breath, it delineates technology and commerce as the principal areas where private universities should offer courses and welcomes foreign direct investment in higher education. When PFRE discusses restrictive controls in government-sponsored higher education, the solution offered, out of that logjam, is privatization. In a departure from PFRE, I think that as a policy option the nation can also explore that government-funded universities could be reformed, ushering in an environment of lesser rules and better governance.

While pushing for privatization, PFRE stresses on equity and social justice. We see a strong advocacy of making education inclusive for the physiologically challenged and a deep concern about the state of laboring population in the unorganized sector. Though texts such as UEC (1948–1949) address the theme of poverty, it is PFRE that categorically points out the huge gulf of economic opportunities between the organized white-collar professionals and the vast pool of unorganized poor laboring population. However, the overarching thrust is for privatization. Nehru-era policy and governing philosophy was techno-bureaucratic; post 1991, the techno-bureaucratic gets replaced by and transformed into techno-mercantile. I say, "replaced and transformed" because the policy does not get replaced one fine morning, rather there is a gradual transformation of policy. I deliberately use the concept of transformation because what happens in post-1991 India is that the beneficiary techno-middle class of the Nehru era, it is they whose ideas get transformed into techno-mercantile. The dominant groups of beneficiaries remain largely same, the classes and sets of people who were votaries of techno-bureaucratic structures before 1991; after 1991, they became votaries of techno-mercantile structures. We see the shift in the pages of higher education policy. With its push for private university, the PFRE reflects this shift and embodies the educational vision of new techno-elite in a new India.

Much Disquiet on the Private Front

Nearly two decades into the liberalization, privatization, and globalization story, in 2008–2009, the UPA government of the time constitutes a committee to give recommendations. "Committee to Advise on the Renovation and Rejuvenation of Higher Education" (CARHE) was chaired by Yashpal, a scientist and professor. It was constituted in early 2008 and submitted its report in 2009. Unlike PFRE, most members of this committee were from academia and a few from bureaucracy. Like its predecessors, CARHE too discusses the problems in higher education:

> Loss of primacy of the universities in the scheme of the higher education sector in India, erosion of their autonomy, undermining of undergraduate education, the growing distance between knowledge areas and the isolation of universities from the real world outside and crass commercialization

> are some of the problems that characterize the growth of the Indian higher education system.

Discussing the ills that have plagued the government-funded university, it severely criticizes the state of private higher education. After two decades of expansion of private higher education in India, CARHE gives us a reality check; it tells us much is wrong in the private universities that have mushroomed since the push toward privatization in early 1990s. As they say in the quote above, "crass commercialization" is a problem "that characterize the growth of Indian higher education system."

CARHE points toward the corrupt and less than transparent practices of private institutions. At the same time, it also notes that the over-regulatory attitude of the governing bodies in higher education hampers the entry of genuinely philanthropic endeavors in setting up higher education institutions:

> The solution to the unscrupulous methods of some private investors should not mean doing away with their participation in the field of higher education altogether. In order to reach the goals of doubling the higher education capacity from the present level, it will be necessary to encourage participation of the private sector.

The report puts forward its unease with private higher education institutions:

> Purely private initiatives require a credible corrective mechanism to do away with the ills associated with it currently. It would be necessary for instance that the present practice of family members who sometimes don't have the experience or the competence relating to education occupying the controlling position of the governing systems of the private educational institutions be prevented. Similarly, the practice of conferring academic designations such as Chancellor, Vice Chancellor and Pro Vice Chancellor to members of the family has to stop.

Continuing its criticism of private institutions, the report urges private institutions:

> not to confine themselves only to commercially viable sectors of education such as management, accountancy and medicine, etc. but should also

encompass social and natural sciences by establishing comprehensive universities.

CARHE shows displeasure toward private higher education institutions for high fees; education needs to be affordable and clearly private universities by charging hefty fees do not cater affordable higher education.

CARHE does not share the optimism toward private higher education that we saw in PFRE. Though CARHE accepts the importance of having private higher education, it shows its failings on several counts. In 2000, the mood of the power elite was all too optimistic about private higher education; at the end of the next decade by 2008–2009, the optimism had faded. The academics in CARHE may grudgingly accept a private role in higher education, but the flaws of the private sector were clearly no less than the ills in the government sector. Privatization was clearly no panacea in the higher education sector.

India's Policy Prescriptions for Bharat

In recent decades, the public world in India has often referred to the existence of two worlds within the same republic: one called India and another called Bharat. Bharat is a name that the landmass derives from history beyond the second millennium whereas India is the British nomenclature of the country. In contemporary times, in the India/Bharat divide, the discourse has pointed out that there is an English-speaking techno-modern affluent India and an English-fearing chaotic rural-small town Bharat. Does this divide sneak its way into policymaking in higher education? I show how the ramifications of India/Bharat shape education policy thinking and impact Indian higher education.

While CARHE shows the problems of private universities, it also critiques the nature of governance in government-funded institutions; universities and the higher education system as a whole are over-regulated, and educational institutions suffer from excessive rules and regulations imposed on them by governing bodies. Advocating maximum autonomy for the institutions, it tells us that while institutions like IITs and IIMs enjoy a great degree of autonomy, the general central/state university is subject to tight administrative controls, which acts as a negative weight on the academic life of the universities.[15] Thus, elite institutions enjoy autonomy; the ones lower down the pecking order suffer from the baggage of rules and regulations. Clearly, there is freedom for India and shackle for Bharat. Within the same broad educational sector, we have a different set of norms for institutions. There is no clear logic apart from the class/elite angle as to why IITs or IIMs should enjoy far greater autonomy than the undergraduate college in a small town. What this regime indicates is that IITs and IIMs whose graduates are destined to fill up the ranks of techno-mercantile elite are hence privileged to enjoy autonomy. The system creates an elite and in that process also creates elite institutions which have a distinctly different set of norms than the ordinary institutions and ordinary student and teaching population that form the bulk of the higher/tertiary education sector.

CARHE laments the existence of too many rules and regulations that weigh down the colleges and universities, yet strangely enough, it wants to create a governing body over and above all other existing bodies, to govern the higher education sector. Will the addition of an overarching body on top of all other bodies add to the quality of higher education dispensed by India's institutions? It was strange that policy planners who are talking about the malaise of over controlling structures are themselves advocating the creation of one more new structure over and above all the existing structures. Here is a desire for India to be in control of Bharat.

CARHE says many more young people are there in colleges and universities today than in past decades, and that they want jobs after completion of education; unlike in earlier periods, education was not a goal in itself. This view is clearly an elitist bias in policy thinking. The young Indian who went to do a BA in English in Presidency, Stephens, or Oxford in 1960s—did she/he pursue it only for the joy of learning?[16] I think that is an oversimplification and a serious glossing over of class character of higher education. Those from India who have had pursued or pursue higher education do that with a variety of motives, of which one strong component is economic/material gain, and cultural/educational status is also strongly linked to material gain. Similarly, for those from Bharat, their motive is not only to get a job; there is surely the job angle but the aspiration for higher education is also cultural. The experience of higher education is multi-dimensional for every young person. To think that new entrants in the higher education scene, many of whom may be first-generation learners, are in the university only to get jobs is a case where India thinks it knows Bharat and can also frame an effective policy for Bharat. Such inaccurate thinking points to the depth of the divide between India and Bharat.

CARHE itself also points to India/Bharat issues. In a distinct departure from earlier policy texts, they point to the isolation of IITs and IIMs. The policymakers advocate that the institutions

> broaden their curriculum framework and assume the functions of full-fledged universities without losing their unique character. We can then look forward when IITs and IIMs will produce scholars in literature, linguistics and politics along with engineering and management wizards who would have substantial motivation for engagement with the local community, and the opportunity to use and enhance learning by solving real-life problems in their immediate environment.

This "local community" is Bharat and CARHE rightly says, unless the elite institutions come out of their isolation of India and unless they are able to think of taking Bharat forward along with India, the perceived excellence of these institutions will always face a question mark.[17] It clearly voices unease with private higher education and shows where IITs and IIMs have lagged behind. Two strands of policy, that of private higher education and of elitist institutions of knowledge, both come under the critical gaze of the policymakers. This report clearly shows the problems with private institutions and elite universities such as IITs and IIMs. These institutions have always been showcased as centers of excellence, but 50 years after their founding, a policy text shows where they have failed. Without saying in as many words, CARHE tells the IITs and IIMs that it was time they stopped being confined in India and stepped out into Bharat.[18]

Translating Policy, Bridging the Divide

CARHE urged IITs and IIMs to step out into Bharat. NKC chaired by Sam Pitroda was initiated by Prime Minister Manmohan Singh during the UPA regime (2004–2009); its policy recommendations too could bridge the India–Bharat gap. Unlike any other policy text, before or after it, NKC was made available in ten Indian languages, a small but extremely important step to bridge the India/Bharat divide. English-savvy India and English-fearing Bharat inhabit different language worlds with a largely different set of cultural lexicon. With NKC, at least, a process started wherein policy texts from the central government level move beyond the English and Hindi confines to getting published in a number of Indian languages. In India, a country of continental character, there are more languages than ten. When a major policy text gets available in ten Indian languages, a signal is sent out that English-knowing India wants to take non-English Bharat along with it in a journey called progress or development. Second, when a document gets available in these many languages, the intellectual worlds in those languages have a very concrete option to engage with policymaking. If this process is institutionalized such that every policy document in education or health or rural development gets translated into a dozen languages, that will definitely initiate robust debate and will pave the way for a richer policy environment and a more effective policymaking.

NKC lays great stress on translations. It advocates setting up of knowledge and information portals on health, environment, rural issues, and different important areas, and it urges that each portal must be made available in all the major Indian languages. The policy makers clearly try to think of Bharat and do not remain confined in India. Even Bharat is not a uniform single shade of economic and cultural opportunities. Tribal populations are the most trampled within Bharat. NKC is the first policy text that clearly urges that learning materials must be made available in tribal languages; this may have also been an impact of the Maoist movement with its support base among the tribal peoples of central India.

The urge to create policy solutions relevant to Bharat is most markedly seen when NKC discusses vocational education. Unlike previous texts which have lamented the sorry state of vocational education, NKC actually points to the core of the problem:

> It is widely recognized that a crucial problem with vocational training in India is a negative association with manual labor.

This is an accurate characterization of the problem. The root cause of the dismal state of vocational education is the Brahminical attitude that looks down upon manual labor and the consequent influence of the idea on large sections of society. It suggests ways in which vocational education can be salvaged, and it could become an important tool of educating large numbers of young people and providing them with employable skills.

The first is to rebrand it as skills education. From 2006 to 2007 onward up until now, we have seen that skills and skills education has become a popular currency in the educational and economic discourse in India. Both central and state governments have been talking about skills development, and skills development centers have emerged across India; institutions established in earlier decades have also rebranded themselves as skills academies. This new initiative has also brought in private partners into the process, which may have already contributed to a modicum of dynamism in the sector. How far this rebranding will lead to education, empowerment, and employment of large numbers of young people; we have to wait a few years for a more definite answer.[19]

Another important suggestion is that any student who has completed school education till class VIII should be eligible to enter a vocational education course. CARHE too had advocated that vocational education be brought under the umbrella of universities. If we can lower the entry requirements of vocational education and, at the same time, offer graduates the possibility of university certification and further educational advancement in the university system, we can definitely create a new value chain in the educational and professional development of those young women and men who have been traditionally termed as drop-outs. The goal of a truly inclusive educational regime must be to bring in the drop-outs.

A third recommendation is the idea of entrepreneurship. Skills training to develop enterprise and entrepreneurial abilities can be a key in rejuvenating the entire sector of what has been traditionally referred to as vocational education. With new branding of the sector, and structures where drop-outs are translated into bring-ins and enterprise taking root in the graduates, a renewal and rejuvenation of vocational education may become a reality in the not too distant future.

NKC's attempt to be inclusive goes beyond the arena of vocational education. It discusses health education and non-traditional management education, and in both areas, it is clear that NKC is trying to translate policy into the real-life situation of Bharat. It points out the problems in health education:

> Over the years, health related education and training has become more urban oriented, doctor-centric and technology-driven.

It discusses the situation of paramedics and recommends the setting up of a paramedical council which would prepare training programs for multi-skill and specialty technicians and oversee their delivery and quality. Paramedics, NKC says, such as compounders, dressers, and laboratory technicians, can perform public health functions such as health education, and such a health worker can be trained through vocational training.

In its discussion on non-traditional management education, NKC points out

> The need for better management in education, health, local government, cooperatives and civil society organizations and so on has been felt. However, the experience of graduates of Institute of Rural Management and Institute of Forestry Management shows that a lack of advancement opportunities in the government acts as a barrier to the success of such programs. There is a need to establish career opportunities in public management, and systematize recruitment and retention policies.

NKC shows a political will to go beyond the beaten track. It conceives and advocates how management education can realistically contribute to a variety of sectors of Indian life and become truly relevant to people's needs. I will go a step further and suggest that the regular management education in IIMs or similar institutions should have an important area that includes management and public life. The very nature of management education needs to undergo reform if management as a discipline were to have a positive impact on the lives of ordinary Indians.[20] This has started in varying degrees in different IIMs and management institutions but is yet to reform the values at the core of institutionalized management education in India.

Educational Democracy in an Era of Brands and Branding

As this book was completing its last mile, another policy exercise happened in education at the central government level. A draft education policy document was released by Ministry of Human Resources Development (MHRD) in mid 2016. Leaving that aside, since India's economic liberalization in 1991, we have three policy texts, namely, PFRE (2000) led by industrialists Ambani and Birla, CARHE (2008–2009) led by the academician Yashpal, and NKC (2006–2009) led by management expert and policy thinker Sam Pitroda.

In 2000, we saw a push for private higher education; later in the decade in the period 2006–2009, we see that ills of privatization are on the discussion table. Alongside, we see that there is a greater push toward educational democracy. However, the trend of India to remain in control of the realities of India and Bharat remains both in CARHE and NKC. Like CARHE's suggestion of creation of National Commission for Higher Education and Research (NCHER), an overarching body to oversee the higher education sector, NKC too, its push toward educational democracy notwithstanding, advocates the setting up of National Science and Social Science Foundation which, the authors say, will have the mandate to oversee the entire higher education sector in India. Both texts lament and critique the over-regulation of higher education sector, and yet suggest the creation of an even higher up umbrella body to oversee higher education. India with its confidence and unstated arrogance of English and techno-modernity wants to be in control of a continent of people whose aspirations can only be met through educational democracy. And that should begin with democratic values in the policy environment.

NKC has also pointed out that universities in India have contributed to the creation and development of political democracy. Both CARHE and NKC have expanded the policy world toward addressing the complex reality beyond the classroom. That educational policy should encompass the world outside English, that lack of English skills should not prevent students to achieve their higher education potential, that vocational education should enter university, and that university should enter the dusty roads and slums outside its walls are a policy set that has the potential to usher in change. All this, however, happens in the larger canopy of brands and branding. While ushering in of private universities is clearly creating a competition between private brands of higher education, the mentality of branding has gripped the policy environment as a whole. On the one hand, vocational education gets rebranded as skills education. And, on the other hand, most Indian universities and higher education centers show desperation to get ranked in international higher education rankings such as QS. What should Indian universities aspire for, to be ranked in the first 100 or 200 institutions in Asia or the world, or should it explore if management as a discipline can contribute to better health standards of its people. Arthur Morgan, member of UEC (1948–1949), had said that when discussing with hundreds of academics of Indian universities, a stranger may not ever know that a single village existed in India. In this era of branding and brand conscious development, the nation's English-educated middle class plunges head on to international rankings. There is little realization that global rankings and semi-global power status can never be attained when large sections of population are poorly fed and where big issues of development remain unsolved for decades after decades. The critical question is, with all the push toward educational democracy articulated in policy documents, will political democracy ensure educational democracy, or will the limited nature of political democracy severely dwarf the educational and life possibilities of the common Indian, for whom destiny has ascribed a nation called Bharat!

Notes

1. In "Western University, Indian Nationalisms," I have discussed the opinion of Indian scientists on science and development, and that stream of thought in turn influenced ideals of national development.
2. For an understanding of Tagore's educational thought, see Dasgupta (2009).
3. In the first half of the twentieth century, especially in 1920s, 1930s, and 1940s, upper-class Indians went to study in England and a substantial number got influenced by Marxism. At home, the CPI and other political parties such as the Hindustan Socialist Republican Association led by Bhagat Singh gained a large following.
4. In post-1947 India, Gandhi and Marx have been the ideological inspirations, respectively, for the Congress (and parties of the Congress stream) and the communist parties. Though struggle for economic rights of the working class and laboring poor forms a major plank in the communist discourse, individual communist leaders—many drawn from upper castes—do not value labor in individual daily lives. Whereas Gandhians do not put the laboring poor at the center of their idea world per se, but they actually value labor in individual daily lives. Gandhi's advocacy of the use of charkha (spinning wheel) each day of one's life is to drive home the importance of labor in daily lives of men and women.
5. The Central Advisory Board on Education (CABE) in its 12th meeting held in Mysore in 1946 had opined that spiritual and moral instruction should be the responsibility of the home and the community where the people belonged. For further understanding, see UEC (1950). I feel that the change of opinion from CABE committee of 1946 to UEC (1948–1949) may have been a result of the ghastly Hindu–Muslim riots

and deaths in the wake of India's partition, in the years 1946, 1947, and 1948.

6. The large-scale devastation caused by the big world powers during the Second World War (1939–1945) made thought leaders and informed citizens to question the ethical dimension of industrial progress. But much before at the time of the First World War (1914–1918), Tagore had harshly criticized nationalism and its aggressiveness in his lectures in Japan and in the USA. See Tagore (1920). Later in 1930s, he alerted the world to the ills of industrial civilization in his book *Crisis in Civilisation*. For Tagore's disquiet with the modern scientific industrial world, see Uma Dasgupta (2009) edited *The Oxford India Tagore*, especially the section "East and West in A Scientific Age."
7. The dominant developmental vision of Nehru and his advisers has been critiqued in 1980s and in the last decades. In the 1950s and 1960s, there were few critiques. One notable voice of opposition to Nehru's mega projects was Kapil Bhattacharya who was the chief engineer of the West Bengal government in the first decades after independence. In a 1961 report, he strongly opposed the building of the Farakka dam. Because of his opposition to these great "national" projects, he was even branded a Pakistani spy. For discussion on his opposition to big dams and the development paradigm of "commanding heights," see Sengupta (1999) and Chari (2016).
8. In 1992, I first encountered the phrase "commanding heights of economy" in a course titled "Growth of Indian Capitalism" taught by Aditya Mukherjee when I was a student of MA at the Centre for Historical Studies(CHS) in JNU in New Delhi.
9. As a middle school boy in early 1980s, I recall that there was a daily program titled *Chashibhaider jonyo* (For our farmer brothers) in Bengali on All India Radio (AIR), Calcutta. I am almost certain that similar programs targeting agriculturists were broadcast by the AIR centers across India, and they did it in the natural language of the region.
10. Soon after the nuclear bomb was detonated, there was talk among the ultra-nationalists that they would take the nuclear ash to far-flung corners of India.
11. Panchayati Raj comes from *panchayat* which is a traditional system of village democracy where five elected elders deliberated and decided on disputes and issues of governance. In contemporary India, Panchayati Raj institutions refer to the structure of democratically elected rural self-government.
12. For an understanding of the relation between politics and the educational development of Thailand, and the exact juncture of development of open universities in the country, see Watson (1981).

13. Thailand has a much greater portion of its population with higher/tertiary education. The country is nearly 100% literate. Countries such as Indonesia and Malaysia are also in the similar league. This advance in educational attainment of South-East Asian nations, I believe, has been possible because in their respective national educational systems, teaching–learning has happened in mother tongues/natural tongues. The advances of educational attainments, economic growth, and quality of material life have been intimately linked to one another.
14. PROBE stands for Public Report on Basic Education, and the specific PROBE report referred here is the one published in 1998 (www.undp.org/content/dam/india/docs/public_report_basic_education_india.pdf).
15. The problem of poor and undemocratic governance in higher education has become nearly endemic to the sector. For an incisive critique, see Chowdhury (2008).
16. This view that students in an earlier time went into educational institutions for a loftier goal than economic advancement will find few takers. In his introduction to a volume, Sabyasachi Bhattacharya (1998a, b) writes, "To the beneficiaries of 'English education' in the colonial regime, education was a means of economic advancement, chiefly through employment in the service of the state and its allied agencies." The same pattern of outcome of educational attainment continued in post-1947 independent India.
17. For a critique of IITs in view of their inadequate involvement with India's democratic project, see Mehta and Sharan (2016).
18. Of course, IITs and IIMs have occasionally shown interest toward the wider society. Researchers in Guwahati IIT, for example, made an innovation that could lighten the physical labor of driving a cycle rickshaw. Among the IIMs, the one in Kozhikode has had a structure of encouraging incubation centers. Centre for Research and Education for Social Transformation (CREST) is born out of such an incubation center. CREST runs a 5-month course twice a year, for graduates from culturally underprivileged backgrounds with the aim that the course will help the student reduce the gap of cultural capital that the student most likely has in relation to privileged students in the educational and professional environments.
19. Anil Sadgopal (2016) has put forward a harsh critique of the "Skill India" initiative of the Government of India. Though I share his view in regard to some of the negative impacts that Indian's globalizing economic structures can have on the nation's artisans and trades, it is better we reserve the finality of our judgment about the current initiatives. The problem in regard to the skills education sector has other dimensions

as well. Government's inadequacy in developing the skills or vocational education sector has resulted in large private corporations and industry bodies taking over the function of skills training in their hands. Partha Mukhopadhyay (2008) has offered a detailed study of this development.

20. For critiques of management education in India, see Bhattacharya (2010) and D'mello (1999).

Recommended Readings

Government Reports/Policy Documents

Education Commission. 1970. *Education and National Development: Report of the Education Commission (EC)*. New Delhi: NCERT.

Ministry of Human Resources Development. 1992. *National Policy on Education 1986—Programme on Action 1992 (NPE)*. New Delhi: Government of India.

Ministry of Human Resources Development. 2010. *Report of Committee to Advise on the Renovation and Rejuvenation of Higher Education (CARHE)*. New Delhi: Government of India.

National Knowledge Commission. 2009. *National Knowledge Commission—Report to the Nation (NKC)*. New Delhi.

Prime Minister's Council on Trade and Industry. 2000. *Report on A Policy Framework for Reforms in Education (PFRE)*. New Delhi: Government of India.

University Education Commission. 1950. *Report of the University Education Commission (UEC)*. New Delhi: Government of India.

Books/Articles/Essays

Bhattacharya, A. 2010. Mismanagement of Indian Management Education. *Economic and Political Weekly* 45 (24).

Bhattacharya, S. (ed.). 1998a. *The Contested Terrain: Perspectives on Education in India*. New Delhi: Orient Longman.

Bhattacharya, S. 1998b. The Contested Terrain of Education. In Bhattacharya.

Broadfoot, P., et al. (eds.). 1981. *Politics and Educational Change: An International Survey*. London: Croom Helm.

Chari, M. 2016. Over 50 Years Ago, Bengal's Chief Engineer Predicted that the Farakka Dam Would Flood Bihar. *Scroll*. https://scroll.in/a/827254.

Chowdhury, R. 2008. Autonomy and Dignity of Teachers. *Seminar* 587.

D'mello, B. 1999. Management Education. *Economic and Political Weekly* 34 (48).

Dasgupta, U. (ed.). 2009. *The Oxford India Tagore: Selected writings on education and nationalism*. New Delhi: Oxford University Press.

Mehta, Mona G., and R. Sharan. 2016. IITs and the Project of Indian Democracy. *Economic and Political Weekly* 51 (11).

Mukhopadhyay, P. 2008. Learning to Work. *Seminar* 587.

Rajivlochan, M. 2008. Reforming Education for India, from England. *Seminar* 587.

Sadgopal, A. 2016. Skill India or Deskilling India: An Agenda for Exclusion. *Economic and Political Weekly* 51 (35).

Sengupta, N. 1999. A Buzzword Named 'Development'. *The Hindu*. http://www.narmada.org/archive/hindu/files/hindu.19990831.05312524.htm.

Tagore, R. 1920. *Nationalism (Reprint)*. London: Macmillan (Original 1917 edition published by Book Club of California, San Francisco).

Tagore, R. 1941. *Crisis in Civilisation*. Calcutta: Viswa Bharati.

Watson, K. 1981. Higher Education and Political Change in Thailand. In Broadfoot 1981.

CHAPTER 5

Class Struggles in Class Rooms: Conflict, Politics, and the Indian University

Abstract "Class Struggles in Classrooms" discusses conflict, politics, and the Indian university. In recent years, Indians have woken up in the morning to news of student suicides. There have been much-publicized cases where college or university students from lower caste/lower class background have committed suicide; many of these have happened in elite higher education institutions of the country. What has prompted students from economically depressed and socially marginalized sections of Indian society to commit suicide? What is the deeper malaise in India's higher education system? Does the malaise stem from and point toward a deep injustice within Indian society? India's universities and its higher education institutions, especially the ones that are funded by the government, have been founded with the objectives enshrined in Indian Constitution, those of justice, liberty, and equality. The higher education system professes to further the cause of education, of enlightenment, of liberty and freedom, and of justice. In reality, the Indian university is a space where injustice continues, on a number of axes of discrimination. Language, caste, class, gender, urban/rural, and physiological disability all of these provide the sources of discrimination. This chapter details the social and cultural experience of students from margins of society in the sites of higher education; it also looks into the nature of control and of politics in the higher education space. It argues that instead of having a transformative role, in most part, the Indian university plays a key role in reproduction of the inequities of the Indian social system. And, finally,

S. Roy Chowdhury, *Politics, Policy and Higher Education in India*,
DOI 10.1007/978-981-10-5056-5_5

the author points out that this becomes possible because of a poverty of politics in India.

Keywords Student suicides · Axes of discrimination
Reservation in higher education · Politics of control in higher education
Parochial university · Poverty of politics

Of Suicides and Silences

The All India Institute of Medical Sciences (AIIMS) in Delhi is India's premier site for medical education, offering undergraduate and postgraduate courses; it is also a large hospital that caters at affordable costs, to patients from a vast swathe of northern India. Each year, around a million students sit for the entrance test to AIIMS and 72 get selected! Anil had got selected as one of those 72 in 2011. He was from a lower-caste background and hailed from a village in north India. When he arrived in AIIMS, almost everything looked foreign to him; he had never seen such a huge campus, so many big buildings, not to mention air-conditioned seminar rooms. He felt lost. His alienation grew over the next weeks. In order to discuss his problems, he sought an appointment with the director of the institute several times. After repeated requests, he failed to meet the administrator. One cloudy day, Anil committed suicide. The suicide triggered news and discussion in media; it led the authorities to sit up and think of ways to respond to student alienation.[1]

This was not the end of student suicides on university campuses. In early 2016, another Dalit student, Rohith Vemula, who was pursuing his Ph.D. in University of Hyderabad, committed suicide. That became a national issue, student activists organized protest meets in different campuses, and citizens took out rallies condemning the callousness of university management that had most likely led to Rohit's suicide. Vemula had left behind a suicide note which was an indictment of casteist and capitalist democracy.[2]

All Dalit or lower-caste students or students from villages, depressed suburbs of big cities, and from small dusty towns do not commit suicide. Yet do they silently suffer humiliation, do they feel alienated, what roles does the power stream of upper castes/upper and middle urban classes play in their lives, and what exactly is the experience of a young woman of 20 who comes from a small town to study in an elite-tag institution in one of India's big neon-lit cities? I did a brief survey, more of an informal set of interviews and conversations.

Shortly after Rohith Vemula's suicide, the Bengali daily *Ananda bazaar patrika* carried an article titled *ami dalit* (I am Dalit) by a young college teacher called Mohitosh Mandal.[3] He tells us his life story and the difficulties of being an academic from the lower caste in Calcutta's famous campuses, often seen as progressive communities. Born and raised in a poor agricultural family some 50 km away from Calcutta, where rainwater leaked through the roof of his house each monsoon and wet his textbooks, he rose through determination to study English literature in a Calcutta university. With excellent academic scores, he landed himself a job as a university lecturer. However, in his journey from village to city, the university world bared its prejudice toward this young Dalit man. In his student days, a professor would tell him, he should not study English literature because it was not for him; another would tell him he should not pursue research in literary theory as he would be a misfit for that. In veiled and not so veiled ways, the urban professor's prejudice humiliated him at different steps of his academic journey. He goes on to narrate that the social upper caste/class prejudice has not left him even when he has now become a university teacher. Now, he faces flak from students; to many of them on the campus, he is an outcaste. To me, it is evident that his non-English-medium school background, his lower-class and lower-caste background, and his rural background, a combination of all four, have contributed to the discrimination against him.

While Mohitosh faced open discrimination, many who do not face it still go through alienation where the causes stem from class, rural–urban divide, and language. Mimi came to study in the big city college from one of the Calcutta suburbs that dot the Hugli River. These semi-urban locales were once throbbing industrial sites in the heyday of industrialization in southern Bengal. Now fallen into disrepair, these towns are decrepit and the social milieu consists of lower classes, lower-middle, and at best middle classes. Mimi had gone to a Bengali–medium school in her neighborhood, was a bright young girl, and found her place in the hallowed city college that she aspired for. Once she was in her first year BA history class, everything and everyone looked alien to her. She could not understand the English accent of the best professors; she did not know the city music bands that her classmates were passionate about, and she hardly knew anyone who had come from a similar class background to study history. For much of the first months, in the college corridors of glory, she was all alone.

This story of alienation is not Mimi's alone. Discrimination and alienation are experiences of a large number of students in the elite-tag institutions; the outcomes are varied. While Mohitosh and Mimi have fought back, everyone is not a fighter. A few years ago, a young student from Malda, a town in north Bengal, got admitted in a literature department in a Calcutta university. A woman teacher in the class ridiculed him and his lack of necessary cultural background so much so that he left the university after a week. One of his classmates tells me he disappeared altogether. So, while we have some small number of fighters, we have many more of these silent disappearances, young bright minds that travel from village or town to the neon-lit academic city, only to be spurned by the culture of power stream to return to their centuries-old state of still silence.[4]

Axes of Discrimination

Moonis Raza (1990) points out, in the 1980s, i.e., four decades after independence, the literacy rate for upper-caste urban male in Kerala's Kottayam district was close to 90%, and that for low caste rural female in Rajasthan's Barmer district was less than 1%. While Dalits were 15% of the overall population, their share of higher education enrolment was half of that figure. These realities of 1980s have definitely changed for the better; the disparities between urban and rural have surely decreased. But the axes of inequities and of discrimination remain. Discrimination results in inequities; inequities fuel discrimination; one leads to another; and the inherent divisiveness in society continues and provides a fertile ground for conflicts, overt, and covert.

What are these axes of discrimination? Language, caste, class, gender, urban/rural, and physiological disability all of these provide the sources of discrimination. English, as I have argued in "Brahmin Language: Hindu Growth," is a tool of power and a new caste marker; its journey started in colonial India, but its stranglehold has increased in the 70 years since independence. Caste contributes both in its literal sense and also expresses itself as a mentality. A caste-fuelled mentality is at the core of much of the discrimination along lines of language, class, urban/rural divide, and gender. Class is the new caste in India. The two merge to create what I would like to call\"claste" discrimination. More often than not, the upper castes are also the upper and upper-middle classes both in rural, semi-urban, and urban settings, while the lower and other backward castes are the lower and lower-middle classes. Gender remains possibly the most deeply rooted area of discrimination in Indian society. While caste is most pronounced in Hindu populations, principles in Islam are against the idea of caste—it is a religion that strongly advocates all men are equal before the Almighty. In South Asian Muslim populations, though caste is prevalent to an extent, its societal impact is possibly less than in Hindu populations. However, gender inequities remain strong in Muslim societies. Of course, women's movements continue to challenge patriarchy, both in Hindu and Muslim populations. The urban–rural divide plays out in more ways than one in exacerbating discrimination. A disproportionately huge proportion of universities and especially the elite-tagged ones are in big metropolitan cities. In a "claste" mentality, habitats too get structured into the four-tier caste hierarchy: metro cities, tier two cities, towns, and finally villages at the bottom of the pyramid. Discrimination along lines of physiological disability probably remains in the worst state. The campaign against such discrimination is weak, and society and university are far from inclusive toward those with disabilities.

Reservation Leads to Downgrading of Excellence in Higher Education?

Nearly, all education policy texts believe that politics on the campuses is negative and detrimental to higher education. Yet, politics and higher education are inextricably linked. In 1990, Prime Minister V.P. Singh, a man of socialist vision, accepted the recommendations of Mandal Commission that had advocated reservation for OBCs in higher education and in government jobs in addition to the already existing reservation for Dalits/Scheduled Castes and tribal populations. All hell broke loose in many parts of India. Students from upper castes brought out rallies, held protest movements, and received front-page attention in newspapers. University teachers joined them in their attempt to save excellence in higher education; they felt that with more reservations for backward castes, academic standards will be badly affected. Passion rose high to defend Brahminical entitlements; in a few instances, upper-caste students took to self-immolation.

The reservations came to stay. The non-Congress government of the day instituted one of the most socially inclusive political decisions in independent India. During the last three decades of India's freedom struggle from 1920s to 1940s, with Ambedkar at the helm, Dalits had found a voice of their own. That got reflected in the making of Indian Constitution and the post-independence reservations for Dalits, who were termed as scheduled castes. Forty years had passed since then; a plethora of castes between the upper castes and the Dalits had found a political voice, especially in the anti-Emergency movement in the 1970s. V.P. Singh's decision of reservation in universities and in government jobs was recognition of that voice in India's many layered political democracy.

Did reservation compromise academic excellence; does reservation compromise academic standards? For the sake of debate, let us assume that reservation and more reservation lead to a downward spiral in higher education standards. If that were so, one would assume that when reservation was only around 20%, i.e., the first 43 years of independent India, Indian universities and the IITs and IIMs must have produced much cutting edge research or at least produced a large number of papers in acclaimed journals or transformed the content and meaning of higher education from what was left behind by the colonial system. And, correspondingly one would expect that in the two and half decades since the Mandal Commission, there has been a drastic downgrading of Indian universities and IITs and IIMs. Neither is the case. Nor did Indian higher education system produce an internationally respectable body of research before 1990, nor has it fared any worse in the post-1990 period. In research output measured through papers published in peer-reviewed international journals or in number of patented inventions, India has consistently lagged much behind global knowledge centers such as Western Europe, North America, and Japan.[5] Under the guise of the talk on excellence, the anti-reservationists were anti-democrats and wanted to continue and still desire to continue today, the stranglehold of upper castes in higher education and cushioned jobs. NKC tells us that only 7% of India's workforce is in the organized sector, i.e., large public and private corporations, banks, and similar big economic institutions. Upper castes constitute around 15% of India's population, and if one does a census of this cushioned sector, one would most likely see upper castes have cornered 75% of these jobs. In the rest 93% of the workforce, we will most likely find 75% or more are Dalits or OBCs. In effect, the societal caste divide reinforces itself through a "claste" divide that invades the cushioned sector. Higher education is the gateway to this cushioned sector. What the anti-reservation lobby signified then and now is an effort at social gate-keeping; excellence in higher education was a poor excuse.

Girls Become Nurses, Boys Become Bus Drivers

The number of girls in schools and that of young women in colleges, polytechnics, and universities have grown manifold from the very low levels in 1947. However, higher/tertiary education acts as another theater for prevalent gender biases which result in marginalization of women. In most of the humanities departments, girl students far outnumber boys, and the trend is some four decades old. It is more pronounced in the largest urban centers. In the sciences, boys are more than girls, and in technology and medicine, they heavily outnumber the opposite sex, and in commerce and accounting, it is nearly a man's world. Nursing colleges attract only girls, while a course to become an electrical mechanic churns out male professionals. It is evident that gender roles are ascribed to girls early in their lives, and one such role idea is that women are caregivers, hence the choice of nursing.[6] Boys are culturally trained to be macho men; hence the nearly total preponderance of men as bus drivers, taxi drivers, auto drivers and the concomitant flouting of all kinds of traffic safety rules. Boys far outnumber girls in law, management, and medicine. While nearly all nurses are women, the number of male dentists is probably 20 times more than that of female ones. The higher education space is one of the core centers where societal biases structured along gender lines are carefully nurtured.

The anti-woman bias within the higher education establishment gets reflected in the composition of leadership within the university world. In positions of academic governance such as principals of colleges and vice-chancellors of universities, there would possibly be one woman for every ten men. What is even more interesting is the leadership of academic societies. Disciplines such as history have attracted more women in the last four decades. But take the leadership of the Indian History Congress; you will invariably see a preponderance of men as presidents, secretaries, and even sectional presidents during the annual sessions of the Congress. Same will be true for the Indian Science Congress. The composition of teachers' union in different universities and colleges reflect the same trend. The university leadership, even if it has a nominal awareness about this state of things, does scarce little to reform the gender biases prevalent in choice of subjects and life-careers of young women and men. And, when it comes to actual leadership, I suspect men actively impede the possibility of women becoming university leaders.

Parochial University?

Writing in early 1970s, Susanne and Lloyd Rudolph (1972) initiated an important idea in the discourse on Indian higher education. They rightly observed that "traditional structures like villages and castes are becoming more cosmopolitan." This trend of late 1960s and early 1970s has definitely gained further momentum, 50 years later. This transformation of the traditional structures of society, they argued, resulted in "university parochialization." They felt that Indian universities were no longer insulated from the pressures of democracy, and the newer universities formed after independence cared less for international relevance of curriculum or reference. They rightly asked, as the universities become more socially and culturally representative, will they lose their cosmopolitanism? Alternatively, can the Indian university induct new constituencies in the creation of knowledge worlds and make knowledge relevant to local needs?

While the Rudolphs had pointed to a key area in understanding the contemporary Indian university, universities have neither become wholeheartedly socially and culturally representative nor have they bridged knowledge and local concerns. As for the former, the stranglehold of claste in universities continues. In Calcutta University, for the first 70 years, its Department of Geography did not have even one teacher from any of India's hundreds of scheduled tribes, nor was there any teacher who was Muslim![7] Positions earmarked for individuals from the Dalit communities were routinely filled up by upper "claste" individuals. So, even the process of being socially and culturally representative has been an extremely limited one. Because of politics, democratic movements, and constitutional mechanisms in place, the dominant groups within the university have paid lip service to social inclusion but have carefully kept the largest sections of Indian society outside the academic clubs. And the creation of knowledge worlds for local needs has not even taken baby steps. Mental resistance, tied up with material self-interest, to social and cultural inclusion within academia has led to the academic inertia toward change that could have created knowledge for local needs. What has happened is that on the one hand, the university becomes parochial by caring less for international movement of knowledge, and on the other hand, it does nearly nothing to make knowledge locally relevant. Where the university has headed in its parochial condition is the poor copying of Western knowledge and parroting it in the worst possible manner for further dissemination.

If we turn to policymaking, there is an important turn to the theme of "parochial university." While I agree with the thrust of Rudolphs, there is at least one area where Indian policymaking was more parochial at independence than 70 years later. UEC (1948–1949) had opined that the natural place of women is in the confines of home, and the policy document was detrimental to the development of women's education. Later documents like the National Policy on Education (1986/1992) strongly advocated women's education, and for the first time, women's study and resources centers were created within the universities. In this regard, policy thinking has moved away from a parochial view of the higher education space. Surely, if Indian higher education before 1947 was more international and yet had no women participants in that process, that internationalization was not democratic; nor could it be an ideal of cosmopolitanism.

Politics of Control in the Higher Education Space

From its beginnings in the colonial era till now, Indian universities have always been tied with politics. There are two distinct ways of the university–politics encounter. One is the founding of colleges and universities and the flow of funds from the central or state governments. The other is the process of control of the university campuses by competing political parties and competing politicians. There is a third element of power within higher education institutions, and that is of a burgeoning bureaucracy/administration.

Since 1947, the central government has been the biggest source of funding to the higher education sector. University Grants Commission (UGC), a body under the central ministry of education, now called Ministry of Human Resource Development (MHRD), is responsible for most of the funding that the state and central universities receive. Predictably, UGC and through UGC the central government tries to control the universities. In covert and at times, overt ways the political party/parties in power use UGC as a tool to control the higher education space. Though there are political issues in the ways that UGC's power is exerted, for the most part, UGC exerts itself in administrative ways where it functions as a mega-bureaucracy. Under this overarching bureaucratic control of UGC, the universities themselves create and nurture their own administrative structures. While the position of a principal in a college is often a seat of power to control the everyday happenings in a college, in the universities positions such as of the vice-chancellor and the registrar assume great power over academic workings of individual teachers. The role that university bureaucracy plays can be extremely demeaning toward the dignity of the academics, and we have seen in recent years, academics articulating their displeasure strongly.[8] The power of UGC or the respective college bureaucracies is about administrative control and show of who's the boss. In the process, the academic world within colleges and universities suffer from a powerful versus victim syndrome.

The teachers organize themselves into unions and while, on the one hand, they agitate about the material conditions such as pay, etc., their fight against what is perceived often as an oppressive bureaucracy is equally important. Those in university governance, instead of providing much-needed leadership to the higher education institutions, become more interested in the show of their little powers. The teachers' movement gets caught into this cycle of protests against the university bureaucracy. The whole cycle of exchanges between UGC, university administration, and teachers' unions takes the university world on a downward spiral. This is a failure of management; with political will, all parties concerned can devise ways of better management and effective leadership of the college and university world.

While this play of power and resistance is from the everyday happening on the campuses, the founding of colleges and universities is in themselves an act of politics. In the colonial period, wealthy Indians formed educational institutions, schools, and colleges. These institutions served as tools for extending their influence on society at large. A second pattern was founding of educational institutions by different sects or specific religious communities. This continues in the post-1947 period, a third pattern gets steam in independent India. Politicians active in a particular town or district either start educational institutions including colleges or reach the position of control in existing institutions.[9] This third kind becomes the most popular form of political control of higher educational institutions. Organized political parties too carry out a systematic effort to control higher education and its institutions. In some states such as West Bengal under the CPI-M rule between 1977 and 2011, the party in power routinely intervened in the functioning of colleges and universities, and especially for the universities, it controlled appointments at all levels. While the CPI-M's virtual takeover of higher education in West Bengal has been much discussed, almost all political parties when they are in power in the states or at the center, they meddle in the daily lives of institutions and influence/control appointments. And this process of negotiation between the political party and the higher education world is finely enmeshed in one another.

The teachers' unions are vocal and important players in the colleges and universities. The leaders of the unions represent one or the other political party and often rise through union activity to the core leadership of the parties. And if a particular party comes to power in a state, the party appoints every now and again a person, who has risen through teachers' unions, as minister of education. The education minister then goes ahead in putting his pals into positions of power. And the rival political party awaits its turn. This forms an important dynamic of the power processes where politics and higher education meet.

Student Unions in a Democratic Society

Political parties speak in one way through teachers' unions and the control of appointments in colleges and universities, and the student unions form the primary face of politics on the campuses. All through independent India's policymaking exercises, educationists and policy proponents have felt that party-driven politics is a negative influence on the academic climate of colleges and universities, often advocating student politics be brought to an end; they have urged political parties to come to a consensus and withdraw from the higher education space. This, of course, is a utopian suggestion. In a society where education/higher education is probably the primary modern marker of social status of an individual and where access is extremely unequal and is a field of overt and covert contestation, it is but natural that political parties will want to extend their influence on the campuses. Moreover, with large numbers of young people in each campus, the higher education space across the nation offers the single biggest concentration of youth. For political parties or for any organized group, this is where they can easily find an audience for their respective political/ideological programs. And historically, it is the site of higher education that has greatly fashioned nationalism and other contending ideologies in India.

While the call for shunning institutions of politics is an unrealizable one, it is important to examine what goes on in the field of student politics. All major parties and even minor ones have a student wing. The National Student Union of India (NSUI) belongs to the Congress party, the Akhil Bharatiya Vidyarthi Parishad (ABVP) belongs to the Bharatiya Janata Party (BJP), the CPI has its AISF, and the list goes on. The central party charts out a program of activity for the respective student wings. And, with some variations depending on the state and the region, the student wings carry out the program as directed by the party. The parties get foot soldiers from the student population and some of the foot soldiers later become leaders of the party. The primary task of the party's student wings is to win college or university elections. Often, the phrase used is "capture the union." In good measure, the parties train the student recruits into vocabulary and mood of greater electoral politics at the state or national level. For parties, student politics is a recruiting arena and a field to extend their political influence.

We see what is there for political parties in student politics, but what is there for students? Why do students, and only a handful among them, join serious union-level politics? In the absence of deep ideological orientations in student politics, what could be the reasons for students when they join politics? In many instances, it is the family's influence. But beyond this, there is a larger dynamic at play. As higher education goes through a period of massification, it draws into its fold youth from diverse backgrounds, a very large proportion of students coming from not so privileged backgrounds. While for a few, cornered within the academic classroom, politics offers a freer space; for many others, student union politics offers a space for moving to prominence.[10] Those who see even further can gauge that political party affiliation can bring them material progress. In a society where class hierarchies are steep, politics offers a way of responding to sense of deprivation engendered by class. In understanding of caste dynamic in traditional Indian society, sociologists have used the idea of Sanskritization, i.e., a process where a lower-caste group attempts to lift its identity to a caste group that is immediately above in the pecking order. In contemporary India, I think, politics plays that function for many individuals. Lower-middle-class individuals, necessarily not from lower castes, find in politics and often in student union politics the first point of entry to a different social status. By virtue of participation and leadership in student politics, an individual from a low social status finds herself or himself in a new position of high status. This represents a neo-Sanskritizing trend in Indian polity. It lends an important narrative to the larger theme of class and caste struggles within the Indian higher education space.

It is rare that student politics has moved away from the folds of established parties. The Free Thinkers in JNU in the late 1970s and 1980s and the Independents Consolidation in Presidency College, Calcutta from late 1980s till now are two important examples. Campuses such as JNU have been politically vibrant; ideological battles have played out in the minds of students through the various generations in the university. In IIT Chennai, in recent years, the Periyar–Ambedkar study circle has challenged the casteist order of things in higher education and more widely; over the decades in some of Calcutta's campuses, student groups have come out in substantial numbers against injustices of state power. However, considering the huge mass of Indian college and university students, this group of ideologically alive ones is a miniscule proportion. Of course, though small they have a larger impact than their numbers when media takes up their causes. There too, though, class biases come to play. A student demonstration in one of Calcutta's elite-tag universities or in JNU gets wide media attention. The moment the protesting students are from a smaller town such as the University of Burdwan, the news trickles down to a four-liner. All in all, student groups working outside the realm of established political party directed program is scarce little. And, even when they may espouse extremely radical positions like the Revolutionary Students Union, they will still be the student wing of the CPI (Maoist).

Poverty of Politics

While policy planners do not like the presence of party politics on campus, it is politics that has given the most important critical input into the Indian higher education system; the decision of the V.P. Singh government of 1989–1990, of implementing reservation for various backward castes, remains the landmark initiative toward social justice since the adoption of the Indian Constitution in 1950. However, discrimination and deprivation continue along multiple axes. In post-liberalization India, the economic policies of parties on the right, left, and center have gradually moved toward an unspoken consensus. In 1990, the Mandal Commission recommendations were accepted; in 1991, economic liberalization was inaugurated, and since late 1980s, private higher education has expanded in leaps and bounds and has largely bypassed the system of reservation. Economic liberalization, economic globalization, and privatization are the three pillars of material life that most Indian political parties accept. Student wings of the parties remain caught in "capturing the student union" mode; ideological struggles especially centered on contrasting economic models for social development which informed students in the 1950s and 1960s are a far cry in educational campuses today.

There are parties like Bahujan Samaj Party (BSP), Samajwadi Party (SP), Republican Party of India (RPI), and others whose stated politics is that of struggle against caste oppression. These parties too remain caught up in an everyday politics where winning elections and becoming the ruling party in a state is be-all and end-all. The ideological struggle against caste or mentality of caste takes a backseat far behind and becomes nearly invisible. While reservation and quotas for the underprivileged are absolutely necessary for the creation and deepening of a democratic society, it cannot be a sufficient measure. There is a need for a larger and deeper ideological battle. Ambedkar had argued for "annihilation of caste." Without a deep and embedded political consciousness of that ideology of annihilation, reservations alone cannot take Indian society toward a fair political democracy, nor can it give rise to an intellectually dynamic higher education universe. In 1950, while inaugurating the Indian Constitution, Ambedkar was acutely aware of the crisis of social justice in India's political democracy. In Ambedkar's vision, there was both the democratic arithmetic of reservation and the longer term philosophy of justice—the annihilation of caste itself. Unfortunately, politics in independent India has not assimilated Ambedkar's thrust of social justice. While social justice movements and parties have emerged, the sophisticated and complex articulation of social justice has remained a faint inaudible murmur. It is politics that articulates its decision in reservation; however when reservation alone becomes politics, then politics loses its appeal for a world free of injustice. The axes of injustices in Indian society are multiple. When Dalits agitate against injustice, they rally their kin but other oppressed groups are not brought into the fold of the movement. For a struggle born in Manipur or Kashmir, Dalits or tribal populations of central India do not come out in solidarity. A million mutinies across India remain dispersed political struggles. A meta-narrative that brings the struggles into a larger rubric of movement against injustice is sorely missing. Ambedkar fought for the rights of the depressed classes or Dalits, but he did not remain contained in that particular history of oppression. That expansive politics is absent in contemporary India; it results in a continuation of injustices in society and in the higher education space, and the protests against such injustices do not coalesce into a sophisticated political–ideological articulation within and without the university world.

Notes

1. Anil Meena, a first-year MBBS student, committed suicide on March 3, 2012. According to reliable sources, between 2010 and 2016, there have been 11 suicides among students and doctor-interns in AIIMS.
2. There has been a flood of articles on the suicide of Rohith Vemula. For an eloquent defense of the ideals that Vemula stood for, see Bhattacharjee (2016).
3. For the complete article, written in Bengali, see Mandal (2016). In the closing section of his article, Mandal talks about Rohith Vemula's thoughts.
4. The experiences discussed here are sourced from interviews done in 2016, with former students of Presidency and Jadavpur universities in Calcutta.
5. All the hype about the excellence of IITs and IIMs notwithstanding, Indian universities remain in a peripheral and marginal position vis-à-vis the world knowledge system dominated by North America, Western Europe, and Japan. See, for example, Altbach (1993).
6. This phenomenon is a proof of the educative function of society, as conceptualized and argued by Pierre Bourdieu (Bourdieu and Passeron 1990).
7. I have learnt this in an interview I did with a professor of the geography department in 2016.
8. Rekha Chowdhury (2008) has discussed in detail how administrators undermine the dignity of teachers in higher education institutions. A guest lecturer in a girls' college in Calcutta tells me how the principal in the college acts in arbitrary ways with complete impunity.
9. To understand how politics and politicians negotiate with educational institutions, see the work of Harold Gould (1972) in the context of Uttar Pradesh and the work of Iqbal Narain (1972) on Rajasthan.
10. Kanhaiya Kumar, the JNU students' union leader who rose to nationwide prominence in 2016, hailed from a remote village in Bihar and neither

did he have English at his command nor did he have the cultural capital that many of his fellow students had in JNU. However, when he became a vocal student leader on the JNU campus, his social stature was greatly heightened and he gained prominence much beyond the possibilities of his modest rural background. In an interview with me, Debalina Ghosh, a former student activist in Presidency University (earlier Presidency College), has pointed out that in the first 6 months of college she felt alienated and kept to herself. But when she entered active politics, she became much more accepted by all students. The experience of politics giving individuals a higher social location will be shared, I think, by a large number of student activists.

Recommended Readings

Altbach, Philip G. 1993. Gigantic Peripheries: India and China in World Knowledge System. *Economic and Political Weekly* 28: 24.

Bhattacharjee, Manash. 2016. The clarity of a suicide note. *The Hindu*. http://www.thehindu.com/opinion/op-ed/The-clarity-of-a-suicide-note/article14017737.ece.

Bourdieu, Pierre, and Jean-Claude Passeron. 1990. *Reproduction in Education, Society and Culture*. London: Sage.

Chowdhury, Rekha. 2008. Autonomy and Dignity of Teachers. *Seminar* 587.

Gould, Harold. 1972. Educational Structures and Political Processes in Faizabad District, Uttar Pradesh. In Rudolph and Rudolph.

Mandal, Mohitosh. 2016. Ami dalit. *Ananda bazaar patrika*, http://www.anandabazar.com/supplementary/rabibashoriyo/rabibasariyo-cover-story-on-dalit-1.291430#.

Ministry of Human Resources Development. 1992. *National Policy on Education 1986—Programme on Action 1992 (NPE)*. New Delhi: Government of India.

Narain, Iqbal. 1972. Rural Local Politics and Primary School Management. In Rudolph and Rudolph.

Raza, Moonis. 1990. *Education, Development & Society*. New Delhi: Vikas Publishing House.

Rudolph, Susanne H., and Lloyd I. Rudolph. 1972. *Education and Politics in India: Studies in Organization, Society, and Policy*. New Delhi: Oxford University Press.

University Education Commission. 1950. *Report of the University Education Commission (UEC)*. New Delhi: Government of India.

CHAPTER 6

Elite Institutions, Dismal Development: Poverty of Indian Higher Education

Abstract "Elite Institutions, Dismal Development" shows how an undemocratic thrust on elite higher education institutions has led to a dismal state of higher education and development. In the last 25 years, since India has experienced reasonable economic growth, the purchasing power and size of the middle class have grown. At the same time, the primary health indicators and the basic education indicators of the country have remained poor, in many instances much worse than a far poorer economy, that of neighboring Bangladesh. While India is always talked about in the Indian and global press as an important emerging economy, the ground realities of living condition of majority Indians remain abysmally poor. India plans smart cities while its child mortality rates are higher than that of most of its neighbors. India's software industry boasts of providing a wide range of services to global clients while roads in its major cities remain potholed and clogged with traffic; it sends machines into space and its biggest financial hub of Mumbai gets paralyzed with rains every monsoon. The state of dismal development can be found in the higher education sector as well. Policymakers continually talk about "the crisis" in Indian education; this chapter points out that the crisis gets louder by the day. The system has flaws, can the flaws be remedied and a better system put in place? The answer to the flaws lies in what the author calls a mentality of caste and a continuation of a system put in place during the colonial era. This chapter shows how an architecture and geography of injustice plagues Indian higher education. Both in the way how university world has been fashioned and especially in the

S. Roy Chowdhury, *Politics, Policy and Higher Education in India*,
DOI 10.1007/978-981-10-5056-5_6

case of disciplines and conceptualization of knowledge, Indian higher education has remained almost frozen at 1947. The author argues that in order to create a robust higher education world, India has to unshackle itself from the mentality of caste and archaic conceptualizations of disciplines. Though the author sees the flaws of colonial structures, he argues that we need to move out of the binary of colonial/national. Educational freedom which leads to a new ordering of disciplines and of higher education holds the key to a just, equitable, dynamic, and sustainable growth in India. A complete conceptual overhaul of Indian higher education alone can lead to a developed India.

Keywords Caste and class hierarchy · Crisis in Indian higher education
Architecture of injustice · Disciplines and underdevelopment
Redefinition of disciplines · Educational freedom and national well-being

In 2010–2011, my usual day was to take the metro from Delhi's Lajpat Nagar station, get off at Viswavidyalaya (university), and from there walk to the Delhi University's Department of Education. Each day when I stepped out of the train hundreds of young university students, would climb the escalator up to the street level. As soon as we were out of the station, I would see a group of young men—their faces filled with expectation to get a new client. They were cycle rickshaw drivers, each one of them was waiting to get a new passenger who he will cycle to her or his college, one of the many that dot the Delhi University's leafy green campus. The young students—girls and boys—were all in their late teens or early 20s. The young men, who ferried them in their cycle rickshaws in sun and in rain, were also between 18 and 30. Everyday, the two realities of youth stared me on the face. A middle-class upbringing where it is given you will go to a college once you finish secondary education. And a lower-class upbringing—most likely also a lower-caste reality—where the maximum you can dream of is to pedal a cycle rickshaw and ferry the sons and daughters of the middle class to their academic glory. As these two Indias jostled in the edu-urban reality of Delhi University, I tried to leaf through yellowed pages of books and journals in the library at the Department of Education.

The year 2017 marks 70 years of India's independence from British colonial rule. It is also 200 years since Hindu College the first Indian institution of imparting Western education at higher levels was founded in Calcutta. In 1858, the first universities with Western education at their philosophical center were set up in Calcutta, Bombay, and Madras. More were formed by the British administration until 1947. And Indians of different political, social, and religious beliefs also started institutions/universities of higher education between 1900 and 1947. After independence, the number of universities has increased. And centers of higher education, perceived as centers of excellence, have also been formed. The IITs in Kanpur, Delhi, Madras, Kharagpur, Bombay, and in the recent years in some other cities are such elite institutions, as also are the IIMs. The Indian Institute of Science in Bangalore, the Tata Institute of Fundamental Research in Bombay, and the Saha Institute of Nuclear Physics in Calcutta are the elite centers in pursuit of knowledge in core sciences. In recent years, the Indian Institutes of Science Education and Research (IISERs) have been created. The Jawaharlal Nehru University (JNU) founded in the late 1960s is also an elite university, and it was a place for social sciences in the first decades of its existence, now though it has departments of natural and physical sciences as well. There are similar institutions in medical sciences, in law, and in a range of other academic/professional fields. All fields taken together, the number of such elite institutions will be around 250. Compared to this, the number of tertiary education institutions—undergraduate colleges and polytechnics included—in the public and private sector will be close to 20,000.

After a growth of higher education institutions spanning around 150 years, and 70 years since policy planning in independent India, it is natural to ask how have the institutions performed, what have they achieved, have they contributed to India's economy, society, and culture, and if so, to what extent. Where have they failed, are their failings because India has been a developing country, a country that has not yet industrialized fully, or are these failings the reasons why India has remained a poor country. If there are failings of the Indian higher education system, where do the failings stem from, what are the relations between the nature of India's political, social, and cultural worlds and the state of India's higher education?

"A Quiet Crisis"

In education policy documents, one discerns a visible disquiet. NKC (2008–2009) says, "there is a quiet crisis in higher education in India which runs deep." A similar concern is voiced by CARHE (2008–2009).

The areas where the policy thinkers see the university failing are as follows: absence of a robust humanistic tradition, inability of integration of work into the university world, disconnect between theory and practice, fragmentation of the idea of knowledge, a depressing examination system, stigmatization of vocational education, and absence of academic leadership. They also point out that the library system in India is in a bad shape, the graduates of some professional institutes such as of forestry or rural management are not being offered adequate career options, there is a dearth of students pursuing mathematics and basic sciences, and the number of students in universities is as low as 10% (or lower) of the population.

They discuss problems; they also advocate measures which can create better universities. There is a thrust toward doing hands-on work within the educational practice as also creating links between the world of work and the university. In their words:

> Indeed, the experience and culture of work represents that core space where the humanities and the sciences meet.

Further, they point out:

> Indian system of higher education has also kept itself aloof from the local knowledge base of the worker, the artisan and the peasant and the real world.

In order to redress the issue of work disconnect and "the chasm between theory and practice," policy thinkers recommend that the syllabi:

> be designed with a view to inducting the student into a community of participant citizens.

They advocate "compulsory exposure and engagement with different kinds of work … and should include both manual and other kinds of work/occupations." CARHE points out that the present examination system tests certain skills of the student but does not test either her abilities to deal with real-world situations or skills required for theoretical pursuit of knowledge. The system is:

> memory-based questioning, with the occasional rote-based "application" question masquerading as real-world problem solving … entrench the student's lack of ability to examine and understand the real world, as a result

of which their engagement with people or issues remains scarce once they enter the world of work, with implications for their abilities as workers and citizens.

NKC draws up a roadmap for the rejuvenation of higher education and knowledge systems; it shows how more students could be attracted to learn science and mathematics; advocate the setting up of web-based knowledge portals on water, energy, education, food, health, agriculture, employment, citizens rights, and other important issues; create "50 national universities that can provide education of the highest standard," at least 10 in the short term of 3 years; give impetus to open and distance education; and address the problems such as medical education being urban-centric. And, to re-energize Indian higher education, they urge vice-chancellors of universities to give visionary leadership.

Policymakers also sound a somber note of alarm:

> And, in some important spheres, we continue to reap the benefits of what was sown in higher education 50 years ago by the founding fathers of the Republic.

With ideals of a great university in their minds, the founding fathers

> realized ... in a social context characterized by a sharp division between the rural and the urban, the elite and the masses, and between men and women. ... higher education was increasingly perceived as a means to overcome caste and class hierarchy, patriarchy and other cultural prejudices and also a source of new knowledge and skills, a space for creativity and innovations.

How far have Indian universities shaped/reshaped the "sharp division between the rural and the urban, the elite and the masses, between men and women." If the situation was such that universities have not been able to live up to these goals and have failed, that could well signal that Indian democracy itself is in peril. Is the "quiet crisis" in Indian higher education reflective of a quiet crisis in Indian democracy, or has Indian democracy failed to nurture Indian higher education toward the deepening of democracy and social justice, or has Indian university world shied away from "dirty politics" and "dusty India" in order to continue what Pierre Bourdieu famously termed "reproduction in education"?

The Crisis Gets Louder by the Day

While the commissions note that only about 7% Indians of the 18–24 age group get any form of higher education, the comparable number for Asia is 15%, and one can almost blindly say, the number is much higher in South Korea or Singapore, not to mention Japan. This low percentage gets reflected in the small number of students in many Indian universities. A large number of universities have student strength in the vicinity of 5000 whereas for most European and North American universities, the figure is close to 30,000. On the one hand, huge numbers of the youth are denied the opportunity of higher/tertiary education; they land up as rickshaw drivers at the gates of Delhi University or as guards at the gates of gated communities of the upper-middle classes and the rich.

Not only does a small number get to colleges or universities. Those who do, what happens to them after they complete tertiary/higher education? In 2013, the West Bengal government was recruiting primary and secondary school teachers. The total number of teachers to be recruited was about a thousand. Four and a half million candidates appeared for the exam.[1] This is an Indian state whose per capita gross domestic product (GDP) is somewhere in the middle of the rankings of the 28 Indian states. And this is in an India two and a half decades after high rates of economic growth since the liberalization of 1991. Through my association with workshops held in AIIMS in Delhi, India's premier medical school, I came to learn that for admission to 72 seats in AIIMS, Delhi the number of examinees who appear in the all India entrance test is one million!

Examinations in India have become a social spectacle worth several sociological studies; often, they have a huge social cost and take a toll on students and parents, and that is a great national loss.[2] Nervous parents expecting successes of their wards line up at the gates of examination centers, educational entrepreneurs set up tutorial shops, and landlords rent out rooms and paying guest accommodations to expectant students studying for various grades of competitive exams to secure jobs or university seats that will lead to jobs.

Oppressive exam culture has its losses. The state of research culture is also depressing. Devesh Kapur (2010) has pointed out that while Delhi School of Economics produced 4.5 Ph.Ds annually in the 1970s and 1990s, between 2000 and 2010, there has been only a meager 1.5 Ph.Ds each year; Kapur reminds us that this is despite the fact that number of economics departments in Indian universities climbed from 72 in 1971 to 119 in 2001.[3] The students who complete Masters in Economics, a large percentage of them, go to universities in the West for further studies or get sucked into high-salaried jobs with financial institutions in India. The Ph.D. positions remain vacant. While the urban well-heeled girls and boys finish masters and leave for the West, those from India's backwaters of dusty towns in the states of Chhattisgarh and Rajasthan, even if they are academically gifted, they do not have the cultural resources to aspire to study in one of India's premier institutions. The production of research at other elite institutions such as IITs and IIMs suffers from these same cultural and socio-economic factors. India's policy thinkers or university leadership has done little to stem the decline in research output levels at India's top academic institutions. Setting up 50 national universities, as the NKC recommended, will not ensure the development of research output and standards. The answers to India's falling standards in research and in higher education lie elsewhere. It is a deeper malaise.

With some exceptions in a few centers of natural sciences and fields such as nuclear technology and rocket and outer space science, research does not show any promise. With the bleak landscape in research is combined the lack of interest in postgraduate studies. Especially in the engineering streams, students get jobs as soon as they finish their bachelor degree and are not inclined to "waste" 2 more years studying. As a result, a large number of seats at the master's level of engineering colleges go vacant year after year. For the nation, this is not only a loss of unutilized educational capacity but it also means that in the absence of engineering students who complete postgraduate studies, there will be a continuing shortage of teachers for engineering disciplines.

As the master's level languishes, the state of undergraduate studies cannot be far behind. The policy reports rightly argue that in the Indian university system, the undergraduate level is looked down upon, those who are regular teachers at the postgraduate level; they do not teach undergraduate students. Further with college teaching caught in the 9-to-1 syndrome, there has been a rapid deterioration of undergraduate teaching. This points to the academic culture (or the absence of it) wherein teachers in most undergraduate colleges come in to their institutions at 9 a.m. in the morning and finish all their teaching assignments by 1 p.m. and leave. This has resulted in a near absence of a dynamic and interconnected educational community of teachers and students in the undergraduate colleges. With a bleak college culture, students in smaller cities and towns often look at undergraduate education as "time pass," meaning they were enrolled in the colleges because they have nothing better to do.[4] A low morale of the students, teachers more concerned with salaries and far less with the state of academic life, an administrative culture which controls more and governs less, and libraries where the librarian's salary is often higher than the cost of books and magazines bought in a year, this is how dismal the state of college education is in most of India. Bypassing this dismal state of publicly funded undergraduate education, private universities have mushroomed in different parts of India. The private colleges and universities—the bulk of them—address the aspirations of youth for higher/tertiary education and jobs in modern sectors of economy but their standards of teaching and governance are almost as bad as the bulk of the public institutions. They add to the dismal state of higher education; they do not alter the scenario.

Let us turn to vocational education. Starting with EC (1964–1966) and right up to the recent work of NKC and CARHE, policy thinkers are unanimous that in people's mind, there is a stigma attached to vocational education. Polytechnics and industrial training institutes continue to languish. Students who do poorly at the school level and youth from poor families are the ones who enroll in vocational institutions. The policy community is rightfully concerned about the stigmatization of vocational education. However, in a society where caste and the mentality of caste play profound roles, it is not surprising that the stream of education where manual labor is integral to the process of learning and to future jobs continues to be stigmatized. Stigma attached to polytechnics, colleges in a dismal state of dysfunction, postgraduate studies stagnating and research output falling in meaning and in numbers. The crisis of Indian higher/tertiary education is loud and clear.

The System has Flaws, Let us Adopt Remedial Measures; it Will Lead to a Better System?

Policy thinkers look at the systems in place in higher education, they find problems that plague the system, and they advocate measures which they believe will remedy the situation and will galvanize and re-energize higher education in India. I summarize here below the recommendations of CARHE and NKC, which embody the policy community's response after nearly two decades of economic liberalization in India.

They argue "...universities have to be autonomous spaces" and add "intellectual and moral" autonomy from political forces is a pre-condition for the development of universities. With autonomy in place, they suggest that to take the university forward and to ensure it performs its academic, social, and cultural roles well, the vice-chancellor of the university should provide leadership.

They note "the fragmentation of the idea of knowledge," and hence, as much as they advocate a robust undergraduate program for each university, they simultaneously argue:

> it would be necessary that the universities adopt a curricular approach which treats knowledge in holistic manner and creates exciting opportunities for different kinds of interfaces between the disciplines.

As much as they stress on dialogs between disciplines, they advocate the university to take cognizance of the real world. Institutions such as the IITs and IIMs, as also others, should engage with local communities and enhance their learning by solving real-life problems. While suggesting such programs for IITs and IIMs, they also would like the universities to do self-evaluation, and when they do so, they should have parameters which are not only academic. One of these needs to be centered upon the transformative role higher education can and should play. Universities need to ask themselves what roles have they played in respect of the inequities around gender, caste, and class.

Alongside these ideas, they also assert that much greater funds need to be allocated to the higher education sector by the union and state governments. The paucity of funds, they feel, is a great factor in the underdevelopment of the universities. They also suggest new structures of governance. Some colleges should be made autonomous or they could also be granted university status. A cluster of few colleges can be delinked from an existing university to which they are affiliated, and this cluster can be shaped into a new university. In this way, the number of universities will go up, and it will also result in better governance of the higher education sector as a whole.

NKC moves a step forward and discusses issues of training. Pointing out that only 7% of India's working force was in the organized sector, they suggest:

> enhancing training options available for the unorganized and informal sector will be critical for enhancing the productivity of … working population.

Linked to this, vocational education finds attention of the planners. Bringing vocational education to the fold of the university will reduce the stigmatization of the sector. An important remedial measure in this sector can be a rebranding of vocational education as skills development. And when graduates of polytechnics or other centers of skill development become successful entrepreneurs, they could help in taking the stigma out of vocational education.

While there has been the growth of IITs and many engineering institutions, the state of education in basic sciences remains underdeveloped. To rejuvenate science education, the thinkers want more students in sciences and mathematics, both at school and college levels. And in continuation, they stress the need for "more quality Ph.Ds." To enhance the quality of life of fellow citizens with the help of knowledge and technology, there is the idea of setting up of national web-based portals in sectors such as water, energy, environment, education, food, health, agriculture, employment, and citizens' rights. In taking the world of knowledge forward and making India a vibrant knowledge society, India's many languages can play an important role. NKC points out to this need and potential, and argues that learning materials such as books in sciences and other disciplines should be made available in different Indian languages.

With recommendations and suggestions covering vocational/skills, undergraduate and postgraduate education as well as directions of research; governance of university and the higher education sector as a whole, the social role of university, the targets that the nation and the university world should have, and a call to rejuvenate the sector, if the recommendations are implemented, it is well possible that the Indian university world will come out of its stupor and will be an engine for innovation, economic growth, and social justice. To assess the plausible impact of the contemporary set of policy guidelines, we should evaluate the impact of policy advocated in the early decades of independent India. It is important to see what were the recommendations of that era and how much did things change for better or for worse, in the many decades since.

An Architecture of Injustice

Writing on Chinese education, Robert Sloss (1981) tells us, "There is in fact no education that is, or indeed can be or ought to be, divorced from the ideology and the political ideas of the society of which in many ways it is the supreme expression; education is perhaps the most intensely political of all the aspects of a society for it encapsulates the fundamental beliefs and the basic social goals of that society." Nothing can be truer; it is the ideology and political ideas of India's privileged classes that have shaped Indian higher education. Though an ideology of social justice informed India's freedom struggle and the making of India's post-independence Constitution, in subtle and at times in not so subtle ways, India's power stream has subverted that ideology and has skillfully crafted India's education/higher education to suit its political and economic needs.

Policy thinkers want that universities should evaluate themselves on how far have they contributed to better the situation in relation to indices of social injustice such as caste or class. What they gloss over is how the university and higher/tertiary education system itself embodies injustice. It is a pyramid where the top 200 odd "elite" institutions like IITs, IIMs, and others receive a disproportionate share of public money as compared to undergraduate colleges or centers of vocational education. In August 2016, the HRD ministry decided on Project Vishwajeet, which aims to put IITs in the top 100 of global rankings, and in November 2016, IITs have requested a sum of Rs. 22,000 crore (3.2 billion US dollars) over a 5-year period from the ministry. How does this figure compare with budgetary allocations to education and higher education? In 2016, the budgetary allocation for the education sector as a whole was Rs. 72,394 crore, of which Rs. 43,554 crore was allocated for school education and Rs. 28,840 crore for higher education. So, what the government spends for the whole higher education sector in 1 year, the IITs want almost that amount of money for themselves in 5 years.[5] The entire higher education system itself is like the four-level caste structure of Brahminical Hinduism. The IITs and the likes including a few select universities are the Brahmins at the top, the bulk of universities are the second tier, the mass of undergraduate colleges (leaving the elite ones aside) are the third tier—OBCs, to use a term from the lexicon of contemporary Indian politics, and the vocational education institutes are the Dalits or untouchables. Along with inequities of public spending, the mechanism of self-reproduction of the urban (bureaucratic–cultural–political–economic) and urbane elite through the choice of one or two undergraduate colleges in each big city creates the basis of this unjust system. The higher education system, far from being transformative, actively ensures the continuation of the inequities in society. The system goes beyond "reproduction in education," I would say, it is education for reproduction.

The vision of higher education in the policy environment since the Nehruvian period of 1950s up until now has almost always had an elitist inclination. Let us see one aspect of policy thinking present in three tracts which are serious and rich in thought. EC argues for the creation of major universities; soon after, we witness the inauguration of JNU. NKC suggests the formation of 50 national universities, which can impart education of the highest level. These directives have led and will lead to more elite-centrism within the university system. In CARHE, there is a push toward making certain colleges autonomous and giving them university status. Invariably, the colleges singled out are the ones which have an elite tag in the public mind. A few colleges in the large urban centers have moved in that direction since CARHE's report—not necessarily as a direct impact of the report. The advocacy of autonomy for a handful of colleges, while the bulk of institutions in higher/tertiary education sector remain under government control, is one more step toward elitism in higher education. The irony of Indian educational thought emanating from the policy texts and from within the university world as well is that there is the talk of university's role in social transformation while in effect, the Indian university continues to function as a reproductive unit of the unjust social, economic, political, and educational order in India. There is architecture of injustice both within the higher/tertiary education system, and without, one complements and facilitates the other.

Mentality of Caste

The hold of caste itself, i.e., the tag to each individual human being at birth whether he/she is from a higher or lower caste, has weakened in India in the last 100 years. It continues to exert great influences in politics, and there are incidents where upper-caste individuals torture human beings from the lower castes, yet I would say the overall influence of caste on Indian society has decreased.[6] But that does not mean that the ideology of caste has withered away. Far from it, caste has transformed itself into new forms and shapes in contemporary India. The mentality of caste continues, and it has developed and made forays into almost every sphere of life in India. To me, there are two distinct components of the mentality of caste. One is the anti-labor, especially anti-manual labor mindsets of upper-caste/class Indians. Often, this also expresses an anti-gender bias. Communist leaders of different hierarchies would always be up in arms against social injustices in public meetings. After the meeting when you accompany one of them to his home, the man will enter his two-bedroom flat, welcome you and ask you to sit down, and will almost immediately "order" his wife to make a cup of tea for you.

The second strand is that of hierarchy. No matter what you do, in the unspoken rules of Indian dominant public world, each stream of human activity has been neatly categorized in the model of the four-tier caste system. In recent years, India has witnessed a mushrooming of literary festivals. Invariably, the power language of English dominates these festivals. And the literary world too is neatly divided into not less than four categories. At the top of the pecking order are the Indian English writers who live in the West, followed by Indian English writers who live in India, then the writers (mostly upper caste/class) writing in the major Indian languages like Bengali, Hindi, Urdu, Malayalam, Tamil, etc., and at the lowest rung, Dalit writers and writers in the marginalized Indian languages. A 2006 survey of English and Hindi language media revealed the extent of upper-caste domination in journalism. "If men and women are taken together, the share of upper-caste Hindus in the upper echelons of the media is 85%. These castes account for 16% of the national population." The survey found there was not a single Dalit or tribal person among top 300 journalists.[7] A hierarchy that embodies and ensures an unjust system permeates university, political party system, media, and the literary–cultural universe.

While hierarchies and cultures of hierarchy have a debilitating impact on vast sections of society, the anti-manual labor mindset has a crippling effect on the economic development of the nation. In the last 25 years since the economic liberalization of 1991, India has witnessed tremendous growth in software exports, and the booming software sector has fuelled growth in private technical education, real estate, hospitality, and in other sectors. But in this same period of 25 years, what has happened with the physical infrastructure of India. The only noticeable change is a few swanky airports and a few thousand kilometers of reasonably well-constructed national highways. There is not a kilometer of road in any Indian big city without a pothole; there is not half a kilometer of sidewalk which has the same surface level, and in every 2 km, you will see heaps of garbage piles at 12 noon each day. Add to this, the country suffers from floods nearly every other year; a nuclear-powered nation does not have the technology of putting up adequate flood shelters for its hapless citizens. The dismal situation does not stop with rural folk in god-forsaken corners of the land. Almost every rainy season, normal life in Mumbai comes to a halt whenever there are torrential rains. The other big urban centers are no better. The list of such areas where India remains an outdated un-modern society is endless. Yet, why do Indians not wake up and find solutions to these problems. The answer lies in the anti-manual labor mindset.

Working in the software industry or the various sub-streams of business process outsourcing (BPO) involves the use of intellectual skills; India and upper-caste/class Indians have embraced them and have made a reasonable success out of them. But when it comes to cleaning garbage and fixing potholed roads and rough sidewalks, then manual labor is required. The leading groups of the society have gone through an education which has ensured that they look away from these "dirty" matters. The educative functions of family, society at large, and institutional education—a conceptual framework enunciated by Pierre Bourdieu—all of that "educate" dominant Indian groups to look down upon manual labor. This leads to the stigmatization of vocational education. Policy texts point out that Indian universities have not embraced the sphere of work or that they have kept the world of the artisan far away. What they do not spell out is that the reason for this is the mentality of caste which expresses itself in hierarchy and anti-labor mindsets. On the one hand, this leads to the complete sorry state of civic facilities and to cities coming to grinding halt, leading to huge losses to the economy. One step further, this is also the reason why India does not become an innovative society. On the one hand, the power stream and the consumer middle classes can depend on cheap labor provided by large sections of the lower castes/classes, thereby reducing the need to create or adopt new technology, and on the other hand, a complete rupture between learning and labor handicaps intellectuals to the use of hands. Without the use of hands, the mind's ability to actually perform physical experiments minimizes hugely. Commenting on the tendency among Indian scientists to do more theory and less experiment, and as a result stagnate in levels of research, the scientist Sabyasachi Bhattacharya (2011) talks about

> a variety of self-inflicted injuries ... important among them is a self-fulfilling Brahmanical notion that activities involving only the brain are superior to those that require the use of one's hands, and that theory is superior to experiment.

An education that does not stress upon and impinge on the mind the need to use one's own hands to do things, takes away from the individual the capacity to innovate through a skilful combination of mental and manual work.

A Geography of Injustice

In the first four decades of independent India, a common plot in many films was a "stupid villager" who lands in the big city of Bombay (Mumbai) or Calcutta (Kolkata), the difficulties of the person and eventual victory of the rural underdog in the neon-lit city. While mainstream Indian films portrayed the village as a backwater and the city as "modern," the Indian university also espoused the same set of values. For the university educated, whose number is still hovering around 10% of the population, the village is a site to be looked down upon. You go through educational institutions and the first thing you learn is to forget the dusty village and the dirty *moffusil* (small town). Partly, the curriculum contributes to this amnesia. More than the syllabi, what does contribute to the educated turning their back to rural India is the educative functions of the society of the educated, the rich, and the powerful.

Policy documents urge the setting up of major and national universities. And invariably, the sites of these, with indelible influences on their knowledge worlds, have been big Indian cities. The Nehruvian as well as post-1990 educational thinking has ignored the idea and ideals of rural university that was advocated by UEC (1948–1949). Nehru's India gave a technological bend—IITs and IIMs embodying the trend, in the dominant elite-centric patterns of university education—and at the same time reinforced elitism. The higher education system in the 1960s onward created techno-elites while post-liberalization of 1991, the system has married technology with techno-commerce efficiently. There has been a clear divorce between elitist ideals of higher education and the idea of rural university addressing issues of rural poor; the rural university has faded into oblivion.

While the rural university has vanished, the agricultural universities have languished, much like the vocational education colleges. Agriculture was much talked about in the Nehruvian era and until the 1980s. On government-controlled All India Radio, there used to be special programs for farmers; the new Indian nation tried to reach out to its agricultural world and give valuable media recognition to their world. However, with more glitter in consumer goods catching the imagination of a twenty-first century "new" India, talk of agriculture, which was never fashionable, has gone into oblivion. And with it has suffered the fate of agricultural universities and agriculture education. The agricultural universities have stagnated; they are never in public discourse, in the English language media, or in the media of Indian languages. Successive governments have paid little attention. India's annual agricultural growth rate has stagnated at low levels of some 3%, and malnutrition in rural and semi-urban India remains a silent killer. While malnutrition and poor health cause suffering to millions of Indian citizens, it also impacts educational and economic growth negatively.

The literacy level of non-scheduled caste urban male is three or four times higher than that of a rural woman belonging to scheduled caste. Yet, the university world and the policy environment conveniently gloss over this reality. In the absence of rural universities and underfed agricultural education, the vast area of India's villages, home to nearly two-thirds of the population—great part of which are lower and other backward castes and poor Muslims—remains outside the higher education map.

The injustice is even worse in districts inhabited by tribal peoples. There may be a rare undergraduate college in a town at the center of an area inhabited by tribal people, but a university will be almost unheard of. Large sections of tribal students feel alienated in the upper-caste/class dominated higher education establishments in big cities. That results in their further marginalization in the education and employment structures. On the one hand, higher education institutions do not go to their lands; on the other hand, when they come to the centers of higher education, they face discrimination and eventual marginalization. In recent years, the racist attitude of Brahminical India toward the people of India's northeastern states have inched its way to the first page of daily newspapers. In Delhi, home to the political elite and to the largest cluster of higher education institutions built after 1947, students from Manipur, Nagaland, Mizoram, Meghalaya, and Arunachal Pradesh have faced constant discrimination, especially from landlords who give out rental accommodation in the area adjoining Delhi University. The worst case was the death of a student from Arunachal which led to public outrage. While the somewhat more articulate people of the north-eastern states have a feeble voice, the *adivasis* (first peoples) of central, eastern, western, southern, or northern India are unable to raise even a faint murmur. The geography of edu-cultural and economic injustice continues.

Disciplines, Development, and Underdevelopment

In *Joseph Anton*, Salman Rushdie (2012) narrates, in England of 1960s, he had gone to his college graduation ceremony with brown colored shoes; he was forced to go back, change into black shoes, and come back to receive his degree. Such was the power of convention. This power has crippled the growth of knowledge institutions in independent India. In the colonial period, when the first Indian universities developed, they taught disciplines such as English, History, and Geography. The structure of the university was borrowed from Britain; the disciplines have been imported from the West, both before and after independence. While all universities have a department of English literature, not even ten have a department of modern Indian literature. If the university is in north India, it would have department of English and of Hindi; if it is in Tamil Nadu, it will have department of Tamil and the English department will be invariably there; in Ahmedabad, it will be Gujarati department and again a department of English. A department of English is common to all universities of India. And each one will also offer a language that is dominant in the region where the university is located. But only a handful will be intellectually vibrant enough to offer a course in modern Indian literature. Moreover, the courses in English literature, and I suspect, in Hindi, and Bengali literatures too remain frozen in the black shoe syndrome.

While Indian university turns its back to the Indian village and marginalizes the vibrant world of Indian literatures, it also remains in a pigmy stature so far as other world languages are concerned. The number of departments offering masters-level courses in French or German will not cross 20 in all of India. The numbers for Italian, Japanese, Chinese, or Russian are far less, and in all likelihood, a department of Swahili does not exist in India. Departments of Arabic or Persian also attract very few students. India's institutional knowledge world has shown little interest in developing language–cultural links and creating networks of knowledge, economy, and culture spanning universes across the world. These trends in higher education not only reinforce cultural backwardness but also have developmental and economic costs. If this is the state of affairs in languages and literatures, let us see the situation in social and human sciences. How are the worlds in History, Geography, Political Science, or Sociology? Students of history at the BA level in Calcutta, Delhi, or Bombay universities learn about ancient Greece or medieval and early modern Europe but they do not learn the histories of their respective regions in the last 70 years. In most universities, history courses will have a component of India, where Indian history stops at 1947. And even for 1947, while history teaching celebrates independence and laments partition, not a single course is offered in an Indian university that is titled "Partition/Independence/1947." Not only that students do not learn about the immediate past—a past which lives within their present—but also they learn scarce little about their immediate regions. In universities in West Bengal, a course called "history of West Bengal" does not exist, nor is there a course on the history of Tamil Nadu in Chennai, and none learn a course called "history of Indian states." However, the impact of politics on shaping and reshaping of histories continues unabated. The renaming of Indian cities or states is one instance of this impact. Nor do history departments of Indian universities wake up to the possibility of studying histories of neighbors such as Pakistan or Bangladesh. As in languages and literatures, so too in history, the study of world civilizations remains at the lowest level. In the early 1990s, the history center in JNU had not been able to fill up a position of professor of European history for a very long time because it necessitated that the incumbent knows an European language well enough to do historical research in that language. That is not all. The history of history teaching in Indian universities, especially in the dominant ones, has also been heavily centered on students' competence in English. The English-leaning educational culture in these departments has successfully marginalized and ebbed out a large number of bright students and scholarly minds who had lesser English because of their non-Anglophone social backgrounds but were equally capable of being great historians or successful teachers as their Anglophone peers. If one stops at a department of political science or of sociology, the picture is nearly the same. A general feature of the learning environment is that of rote learning; teachers teach from and hand out "notes"—they or their predecessors or their predecessors had taken notes from a famous history/sociology/English textbook, and the notes continue. And, the same dominance of English, the ebbing out of those with less English, the absence of the living currents of Indian society and politics and a teaching culture that "educates" the student away from the "immediacies" of her environment. As a result, a vast number of students, especially from underprivileged backgrounds, cannot relate to the subjects being taught within the classroom. The knowledge of French revolution does not help her to understand why there is an increasing spiral of violence in Indian towns and cities. The alienation of the student from what she learns is evident from an anecdote of a Calcutta college, related to me by a friend. In an oral examination, a history teacher asked in Bengali to a student, "what are the salient features of the capitalist system?" The student replied in earnest—"Sir, I am from a poor family, I do not know anything about the system of money." (In Bengali, capitalist system translates as monetary system.) The teacher failed the student and lamented to my friend the sorry state of higher education.[8] What he or the huge majority of teachers and professors in colleges and universities fail to realize is that it is theirs and the educational system's failure. It is the teachers who are to blame that their teaching and what and how they teach are delinked from the world of the student.

Barring cosmetic changes, syllabi nearly unchanged for half a century or more, teaching in a language alien to a vast proportion of students, rote learning as the dominant form, absence of any encouragement to rigorous questioning and of breaking new grounds, not to mention a complete disconnect between the real world and the classroom, that is, how Indian college education in humanities and social science is 70 years since independence. A poor level of college education interwoven with societal patterns of gender roles results in a huge number of women graduates not entering professions; they stay or are culturally forced to stay within the confines of households; they could have filled up much-needed positions of teachers in the expanding primary, secondary, and tertiary education or could have been successful executives and managers in different sectors of the economy. Dominant cultural forces and poor educational/economic planning lead to "brain-waste" within the country while policy environment at the most talks about brain drain to foreign shores. The dismal educational cultures of departments of history, sociology, and political science ensure that there are less of good teachers and scholars in the respective disciplines; a similar impact in geography, economics, and psychology is of much greater consequence to the nation.

These latter disciplines are more of an applied kind. The pattern of the educational culture being same for these disciplines, there are greater and more direct economic and developmental costs to the nation. If geography departments produce less geography teachers and lesser competent geographers, the society's ability to grapple with floods and droughts and climatic changes and calamities is far less. Though geography is where the development of human geography has led to some interesting encounters between the university world and the "real" world, even if that has had little impact on undergraduate teaching. While India has produced famous economists, the discipline's contribution to areas such as rural economics or economics of labor remains low. The impact of underdevelopment of a knowledge discipline and an absence of effective and socially sensitive teaching is greatest in the field of psychology. Recent studies have shown that India has a high proportion of people with psychological stress. This malaise is a slow killer. Millions of people, poor and affluent, go through severe depressions, not to speak of disorders of higher magnitude. It is neither talked about vigorously nor is there any societal effort to tackle the phenomenon. Another growing phenomenon is youth violence. To tackle these, the nation badly needs a large body of psychologists and psychiatrists. But the discipline of psychology has remained stunted in India. Psychology is an applied discipline. If you were to practice it, you will need to talk to your patient in her language which is Hindi, Tamil, Oriya, etc. If you have been trained in a knowledge universe with English and Western case studies as dominant motifs, you will have a poor ability to relate to the patient. So, the damage is compounded in a discipline such as psychology. The phenomena of depression and of youth violence cut across psychology, sociology, economics, and more disciplines in the social sciences and humanities. This creates the opportunity to create new areas of knowledge and of teaching where different disciplines can contribute meaningfully. The measurable and immeasurable costs of depression to family economies and to the national economy are quite high. However, the Indian university is ill prepared to fashion or even attempt to fashion a response to such issues of national importance.

Psychology–psychiatry is one of the many bridges between social sciences and medicine. The teaching of medical sciences too is plagued often with the same ailments as in social sciences. English domination continues. And the medical establishment nurtures the tendency to turn its back to hapless poor patients. As part of Centre for Research in Education and Social Transformation (CREST), I have had the opportunity to interact with doctor-teachers of the AIIMS in New Delhi. In a CREST workshop, one of our colleagues had asked teachers (who teach undergraduate students of medicine) to do a strength, weakness, opportunity, threat (SWOT) analysis of AIIMS as a medical institution. One participant said that the high number of patients, especially in the Out Patient Department (OPD), is a threat for doing better work. I intervened in the discussion and pointed out to him that the large number of medical cases—which is possible only because there are "too many" patients—can be seen as asset to study multiplicity and variations of ailments. What he sees as a threat, an enterprising student of medicine from a different cultural framework can see it as an opportunity. As with other disciplines, here too, the medical establishment raises walls between itself and the very people who the establishment is supposed to serve.

This great wall of Indian higher education continues to the technology disciplines too. When bright middle/upper-middle-class girls and boys study at IITs, in an electrical engineering class, they never interact with a lowly neighborhood electrician who fixes electrical problems in a household. As a result, both the world of knowledge and that of work suffer. The mentality of caste weighs heavy on Indian higher education, and a flawed socio-educational culture leads to a stunted growth in education and dismal national development. While knowledge and university as its institutional home can be a banyan tree, the Indian university has remained a bonsai.

Educational Freedom and National Well-being

An un-freedom shackles the Indian institutional knowledge world. The import of the university structure and the structures of disciplines from Europe and the copycat functioning of these are now nearly 200 years old. However, there are strong critiques of these in modern Indian thought. Gandhi and Tagore, in different and yet complementary ways, showed how the system of education defeated the purpose of education. From schools to colleges to universities, the malaise was clear. Tagore felt that in Europe education was an integral part of the society's life:

> It grows, develops, and circulates in society, and leaves its imprint on what people say, think and do in their everyday life ... But the schools in our country, far from being integrated to society, are imposed from outside ... There is nothing in common between the lessons the pupils cram up ... and the country where they live; no agreement, but many disagreements, between what they learn at school and what their parents and relatives talk about at home.

He felt Indian educational institutions copied from their European counterparts and, as with most cases, remained poor imitations and lost the central meaning of the European institutions:

> ...English models usurp the whole field of our vision and obscure the achievements of our own country. Even in our keenest struggles for freedom from British rule we remain fettered to Britain in so far as we seek no political models other than the British.[9]

Tagore's critique of the educational system, and of the political and educational cages being intermeshed, is in the same spirit as of Gandhi. While they pointed out the un-freedom in politics and in education, Ambedkar, the principal architect of India's post-1947 Constitution, stressed on the un-freedom in society. The persistence of social injustice and hierarchy fed into and nurtured the continuation of the un-freedoms in politics and education quite well. Such critiques of the system informed India's freedom struggle and the public world of India in the first half of the twentieth century. Yet, not much has changed 70 years from then. Why and how did the desired change fail to happen? Tagore built educational institutions where nature's splendor, labor, and esthetics were central to education; Gandhi articulated an educational ideal with rural life at its center, and UEC urged the setting up of rural universities and colleges, and stressed that the university world should work to lessen the hardships of the laboring poor. However, this thought universe was elbowed out by a vision of "commanding heights of economy" propounded by Prime Minister Nehru. In the 1950s, he articulated this vision where big industries and large infrastructure projects like big dams, power plants, and steel factories were seen as saviors to a poor nation. And to fuel these "commanding heights of economy," he envisioned commanding heights of education. The elite educational institutions of 1950s and 1960s later reinforced the already existing elitist nature of Indian higher education that was founded in the colonial period. Far from a break with the un-freedom in education, Nehru and his upper-middle-class advisers fashioned an educational policy and a political economy that favored the upper castes/classes, marginalized three-fourths of the nation and successfully turned the power elite's back to the vision of rejuvenation of education and society emanating from Ambedkar, Gandhi, and Tagore. In the process, the Brahminical upper-class/caste hold on Indian higher education continued from colonial period to post-1947 India. The un-freedoms in education and in politics that Ambedkar, Gandhi, and Tagore challenged have been reinforced in newer ways. Without any rejuvenation in education, India developed a poor higher education structure which contributed to a thin slice of the population enriching itself and its self-styled good living, while the nation at large remained in a state of dismal development.

One could argue that the policy of upper-class/caste domination of education, economy, and politics has worked well for the power stream; Indians have gone to space, the nation has nuclear bombs, and the GDP has been growing at an average of 6–8% for nearly two decades. As I have discussed earlier, poor higher education results in poor material conditions and ill preparedness of societal challenges; moreover, the myopic vision in education and national life exposes a poverty of imagination. It was the social–political–literary imagination of Ambedkar–Gandhi–Tagore that gave a foundation for a new India in 1947. That imagination dreamt of a strong resilient India where each citizen could flourish to her full colors. That imagination also had and has the possibility of a truly strong India and not a caricature which has nuclear bombs and whose cities get flooded and stranded in every rainy season. To unleash the just freedoms of 1.25 billion Indians, the university world needs to unshackle itself from its own un-freedoms. It needs to break out of, what I call, the "black shoe syndrome" and the "great wall syndrome." A freer world in higher education can lead to a much higher level of material life for every Indian villager and urban-dweller. It can unshackle universities from their pigmy status, unleash new disciplines born in the dirty, dusty world of contemporary India, and lead to greater national well-being.

How will this new education and new disciplines look like? In terms of the institutional ecosystem, the four-tier caste structure of the higher/tertiary education needs to be reduced to three or two tiers. The undergraduate colleges have so far taught physics and history; let them start offering courses in plumbing and electrical craftsmanship as well. The high walls between what is taught in the colleges and in the vocational institutes need to be brought down. The vocational institutes should have teachers, at least one to begin with, who offers a course in liberal arts. The undergraduate colleges, especially the elite-tag ones, need to embrace the world of work. With vocational courses being offered within their walls, they will give much overdue critical recognition to the courses and the students who study the courses. Similarly, students in vocational institutes will be exposed to history, literature, and arts. If pursued with vigor, this step can reduce the gulf between the two systems—one steeped in Brahminical upper caste and the other embodying the lower castes of knowledge and everyday practice. There must also be active linkages between the university departments and undergraduate colleges, and between the elite-tag centers of excellence such as the IITs and the universities and the colleges. The whole endeavor should be toward dilution of the caste mentality-based four-tier hierarchy within the higher/tertiary education universe.

India's reality should inform the creation and development of new disciplines. For example, if a college department in Bangalore offers BA in English literature, then let the syllabus include at least two full courses: one that focuses on translations of Indian literature available in English and another on English literatures in the former colonies of Britain. Both these courses will have the possibility of opening up young minds to two distinct yet connected political–cultural worlds: one world of the many literatures of India and the sub-continent where the changing social realities of life in contemporary India gets expression, and another world where English transforms itself in exciting ways as it grows in post-colonial societies. Such courses will lead to a new politics in literature studies and create the awareness of non-Eurocentric universe in young Indians. Political decolonization may have found expression in a particular way in 1947. But the decolonization of mind is still a far way off; at times, the architecture of knowledge practices in contemporary India even enacts a recolonization of mind. Hence, it is an urgent business for the knowledge world of India to take the first decisive steps toward a new architecture of knowledge.

This new architecture needs to spread its wings to the study of Hindi, Bengali, or Malayalam literatures too. The syllabi in these are often heavily dominated by the writings of upper-caste/class Indians and of men. The syllabus of a Bengali or a Hindi department in a college/university must include courses where Dalit writing, writing by women, and literary expressions from other marginalized worlds come into the classroom. The histories and geographies of injustice need to be mirrored in the texts that fill up minds of young Indians. A critical awareness of social injustices and class/caste conflicts will give a new grounding to the study of literature in Indian languages. Additionally, these syllabi should also move out from Bengali or Telugu insularity and include translations from different Indian literatures and world literatures in the BA and MA syllabi. So, the overall philosophy of each literature discipline should be to break out of the insularity of class/caste and also the insularity of specific language nationalism.

The study of history should also move out of its own "black shoe syndrome." For long years, Indian history has been categorized as Hindu period, Muslim period, and British period. The "secularist" historians will want to break out of this categorization where ancient India is seen as Hindu, medieval India as Muslim, and modern India as British. I feel that the binary debate between the orthodox historians and the modernist/secularist historians won't be able to resolve this problem. What we need to do is to get out of this "black shoe syndrome" altogether. History learning can be reformulated in courses that are titled, and study: power, women, material life, and several other themes. If the rubric of learning itself is changed, then we will conceptualize new courses. A break from sterile binary debates and from a geographical myopia is urgent.

The influence of British, American, or European schools of thought on Indian sociology is well accepted. Recent scholarship (Jangam 2015; Kumar 2016) has critiqued the dominant practices of history and sociology in India for their upper-caste biases. I feel that even sociology's engagement with the dirty, dusty Indian world is much less than what is possible. Apart from a disconnect with the continually changing society in rural, semi-urban, and urban India, what sociology syllabi lack is a study of modern Indian thinkers who have written extensively on Indian society. For example, I doubt there is any Indian sociology department that devotes a significant part of a course on the sociological writings of Rabindranath Tagore. Even Ambedkar's texts are not central in the study of sociology at the BA or MA levels. It is urgent that the sociology departments enmesh the learning–teaching process with dirty, dusty world of India and bring Indian social thinkers into the world of the young college-goers of today.

In psychology, the teaching should gear itself toward Indian realities, and themes such as the impact of poverty and of dominant ideologies such as caste ideology on Indian psyche should come into the classroom. Moreover, as much as translations of Indian literature need to fill up literature classrooms, the psychology departments need to translate major psychology texts into Indian languages so as the practitioners have a vocabulary to communicate with their patients. The need for translations, of course, cuts across all disciplines taught in the Indian university. The process of informing the disciplines with the dusty chaotic realities of India runs from psychology to law to management. What I am advocating can be construed easily as an attempt to Indianize disciplines. However, the quest I have in mind and the one that I have put forward in some measure is not one of Indianization. It goes a little further than that. Since Indian higher education and India's society and politics are my fields of discussion, hence, it may seem I am giving a call for Indianization. The essential aspect of the call is that disciplines that emerged in a specific historical period in Western Europe need to be rethought and reconceptualized in a different global prism of today. The act of rethinking syllabi in Indian colleges and universities is a step toward a redefinition of disciplines themselves. In fact, in several European and North American university systems, new disciplines are being born. Societies in the global south such as India need to take an altogether fresh look at what constitutes each area of study and how the disciplines can relate to socio-political realities and give new meanings to the existence of knowledge institutions that developed under a colonial system that has long lost its significance. And such an endeavor must cut across disciplines in humanities, social sciences, business, physical sciences, medicine, technology, and all other fields of education. The political and intellectual inputs arising from injustice and conflict, the reshaping of academic pursuit through breaking down of the "great wall syndrome," and the complete overhaul in syllabi can shake up the Indian university from its stupor and stagnation and have the potential of unleashing a creative knowledge universe which addresses injustice and practices autonomy of knowledge, while contributing meaningfully to the nation's well-being, world knowledge, and global peace and understanding.

Notes

1. In an article (Roy Chowdhury 2013) written at the time I had discussed the crisis of educated unemployed in India.
2. An editorial in Economic and Political Weekly (EPW Editorial 2016) has outlined the social and psychological costs of the pressure on young people to "crack" entrance tests for elite educational institutions. A detailed study can hopefully bring out the extent of the national loss of the debilitating culture of exams.
3. See Kapur (2010). Kapur has pointed out how far behind India has fallen compared to China's accomplishment in research. According to him, "The contrast with China is stark. In the last two decades, the number of PhDs in science and engineering (S&E) in India increased by around 50% (from 4007 in 1985 to 6318 in 2003), whereas in China, the numbers increased from a tiny 125 in 1985 to 12,238 in 2003 and 14,858 in 2004."
4. Craig Jeffrey (2010) has studied the sociology and politics of "time pass" in the north Indian city of Meerut. What is importsant to note here is that a bleak tertiary education landscape creates wasted youth.
5. Newspaper reports and analysis give a detailed picture. See Chopra (2016), Vishnoi (2016), and Express Web Desk (2016).
6. In the 1960s two decades after independence, two outstanding social scientists (Rudolph and Rudolph 1972a, b) had observed, "traditional structures like villages and castes are becoming more cosmopolitan."
7. See a report published in The Hindu (2006).
8. Siddhartha Dasgupta, who teaches history in a Calcutta college, narrated the incident to me.
9. See Dasgupta (2009).

Recommended Readings

Government Reports/Policy Documents

Education Commission. 1970. *Education and National Development: Report of the Education Commission (EC)*. New Delhi: NCERT.

Ministry of Human Resources Development. 1992. *National Policy on Education 1986—Programme on Action 1992 (NPE)*. New Delhi: Government of India.

Ministry of Human Resources Development. 2010. *Report of Committee to Advise on the Renovation and Rejuvenation of Higher Education (CARHE)*. New Delhi: Government of India.

National Knowledge Commission. 2009. *National Knowledge Commission—Report to the Nation (NKC)*. New Delhi.

Prime Minister's Council on Trade and Industry. 2000. *Report on A Policy Framework for Reforms in Education (PFRE)*. New Delhi: Government of India.

University Education Commission. 1950. *Report of the University Education Commission (UEC)*. New Delhi: Government of India.

Books/Articles/Essays

Bhattacharya, Sabyasachi. 2011. Indian Science Today: An Indigenously Crafted Crisis. *Social Research* 78 (1): 255–280.

Bourdieu, Pierre, and Jean-Claude Passeron. 1990. *Reproduction in Education Society and Culture*. London: Sage.

Broadfoot, Patricia, et al. (eds.). 1981. *Politics and Educational Change: An International Survey*. London: Croom Helm.

Chopra, Ritika. 2016. IITs Estimate it will cost Rs. 22,000 Crore to Improve Global Rankings. *The Indian Express*, 15 November 2016. http://indianexpress.com/article/education/proposals-submitted-to-govt-iits-estimate-cost-of-improving-global-rankings-rs-22000-crore-4375827/.

Dasgupta, Uma (ed.). 2009. *The Oxford India Tagore: Selected Writings on Education and Nationalism*. New Delhi: Oxford University Press.

EPW Editorial. 2016. Killing Children of the Middle Class. *Economic and Political Weekly* 51 (2): 7–8.

Express Web Desk. 2016. Union Budget 2016: Mixed Reaction from Education Sector. *The Indian Express*, 1 March 2016. http://indianexpress.com/article/education/union-budget-2016-education-sector-analysis/.

Jangam, Chinnaiah. 2015. Politics of Identity and the Project of Writing History in Postcolonial India: A Dalit Critique. *Economic and Political Weekly* 50 (40): 63–70.

Jeffrey, Craig. 2010. Timepass: Youth, Class, and Time Among Unemployed Young Men in India. *American Ethnologist* 37 (3): 465–481.

Kapur, Devesh. 2010. Indian Higher Education. In Clotfelter.

Kumar, Vivek. 2016. How Egalitarian is Indian Sociology? *Economic and Political Weekly* 51 (25): 33–39.

Roy Chowdhury, Sunandan. 2013. Uchchho shikshar babu-brittanto: 45 lokkho shikshito bekar! *Ei samay*, 3 April 2013.

Rudolph, Susanne H., and Lloyd I. Rudolph (eds.). 1972a. *Education and Politics in India: Studies in Organization, Society, and Policy*. New Delhi: Oxford University Press.

Rudolph, Susanne H., and Lloyd I. Rudolph. 1972b. The Political System and the Educational System: An Analysis of Their Interaction. In Rudolph and Rudolph.

Rushdie, Salman. 2012. Joseph Anton. London: Jonathan Cape.

Sloss, Robert. 1981. Ideology and Politics in Chinese Education. In Broadfoot.

The Hindu Special Correspondent. 2006. Upper castes dominate national media, says survey in Delhi. *The Hindu*, 5 June 2016. http://www.thehindu.com/todays-paper/tp-national/upper-castes-dominate-national-media-says-survey-in-delhi/article3115113.ece.

Vishnoi, Anubhuti. 2016. MHRD's new project Vishwajeet aims to put IIT in top league of global rankings. *Economic Times*, 10 August 2016. http://economictimes.indiatimes.com/industry/services/education/mhrds-new-project-vishwajeet-aims-to-put-iit-in-top-league-of-global-rankings/articleshow/53626151.cms.

CHAPTER 7

Conclusion: Toward a Democratic Higher Education

Abstract The concluding chapter, "Toward a Democratic Higher Education," points out that India is a political democracy and states that in the picture sketched in the book, the Indian university and higher education universe emerge as an undemocratic institution in a political democracy. The author says, however flawed political democracy may seem, it is still the system that addresses—in a very partial sense, the great inequities and injustices that plague everyday life in India, whereas Indian university addresses those same inequities and injustices far less, and its middle-class inhabitants have failed Indian democracy. The author sums up the book and says that he has explored a particular theme of Indian higher education and development in each of the five main chapters that constitute this book. "Brahmin Language, Hindu Growth" is a look at English and the politics and power around it in colonial and post-colonial India. The specifics of Indian nationalism, the crafting of the nation-state, and the roles of Indian universities and the class that constituted the university in the colonial era are explored in the chapter titled "Western University, Indian Nationalisms." The following chapter fleshes out the developmental visions of the Indian power elite from independence in 1947 till now, and while doing so shows the linkages between world politics and ideas and ideals in Indian higher education and development. These three chapters together bring out a central point. English language, Indian university, the specific fashioning of Indian nation by the English-knowing class, the continuation of the state structure of colonial India into post-colonial India, the particular

S. Roy Chowdhury, *Politics, Policy and Higher Education in India*,
DOI 10.1007/978-981-10-5056-5_7

developmental vision of this English educated, university groomed, state-centered, nation believers all of these have coalesced to give shape to Indian higher education and the state of economic and cultural development in independent India. The specific nature of this development has meant that 10–15% of the population, largely university educated, have enjoyed 90% of the spoils of economic and cultural growth in the last 70 years of India while the vast majority of 80% remain little educated and make do with poor living standards, if not extremely harsh ones. It has also meant that a myopic policy world that tries to ensure the interests of the tiny elite does that even at times, to the peril of the elite itself. Two other chapters, namely, "Class Struggles in Classrooms" and "Elite Institutions, Dismal Development," show what has gone wrong in the pattern of development that was sketched in the first three chapters. The book ends with a call to break out of the continuing colonial knowledge structures and of the elitism and myopia of India, and reorient higher education and development so that the other India that is English-fearing, lower caste, lower class, rural, semi-urban, often referred to as Bharat could be brought into the fold of India and its higher education universe.

Keywords Power language · Power institutions · Science as power
Oppressive power of policy · Non-colonized education
Developmental futures

India is a political democracy. In the picture I have sketched, the Indian university and higher education universe emerge as an undemocratic institution in a political democracy. The systems of political democracy in India are far from perfect, and the challenges of instilling adequate democratic governance in the systems that be, are many. However flawed political democracy may seem, it is still the system that addresses—in very partial sense—the great inequities and injustices that plague everyday life in India. Indian university, I think, addresses those same inequities and injustices far less, and its middle-class inhabitants have failed Indian democracy. The class that benefitted from university and higher education has let India down; it is this class that has let large parts of India remain poor, impoverished, and institutionally uneducated. As for this university class, they themselves have remained happy with improved material riches and a second- or third-class status in the global knowledge universe.

I have explored a particular theme of Indian higher education and development in each of the five main chapters that constitute this book. In "Brahmin Language, Hindu Growth," I look at English and the politics and power around it in colonial and post-colonial India. I explore the specifics of Indian nationalism, the crafting of the nation-state, and the roles of Indian universities and the class that constituted the university in the colonial era in the chapter titled "Western University, Indian Nationalisms." In the following chapter, I flesh out the developmental visions of the Indian power elite from independence in 1947 till now, and while doing so, I show the linkages between world politics and ideas and ideals in Indian higher education and development. These three chapters together bring out a central point. English language, Indian university, the specific fashioning of Indian nation by the English-knowing class, the continuation of the state structure of colonial India into post-colonial India, and the particular developmental vision of this English-educated, university groomed, state-centered, nation believers all of these have coalesced to give shape to Indian higher education and the state of economic and cultural development in independent India. The specific nature of this development has meant that 10–15% of the population, largely university educated, have enjoyed 90% of the spoils of economic and cultural growth in the last 70 years of India while the vast majority of 80% remain little educated and make do with poor living standards, if not extremely harsh ones. It has also meant that a myopic policy world that tries to ensure the interests of the tiny elite does that even at times, to the peril of the elite itself. Two other chapters, namely, "Class Struggles in Classrooms" and "Elite Institutions, Dismal Development," show what has gone wrong in the pattern of development that was sketched in Chaps. 2, 3 and 4.

Power Language

English came to India with the Christian missions. The first educational encounters between Europeans and Indians were centered on teaching of English and dissemination of Christian principles. In the early period of British domination, the colonial rulers held Indian/oriental knowledge and languages in high esteem and were favorably disposed toward teaching of and in Persian, Sanskrit, Bengali, and Tamil. In the

1820s, the elite sections of Indian society, the school book societies in Calcutta and Bombay as important vehicles, started to push for English as the medium of education. In 1835 with Macaulay's distinct articulation and Viceroy Bentinck's administrative ruling, the colonial government gave the strongest and decisive push for use, and if I may add, misuse, of English language in Indian education and development. The preeminence of English has been challenged in policy documents in colonial India, as also by sections of Indian elite. During the freedom struggle, two visionaries with contrasting views of the use and abuse of English championed the use of Indian languages and challenged the Anglophonic hegemony. They were Gandhi and Tagore.

However, the inheritors of Gandhi and Tagore did not quite internalize their critiques of the abuse of English in India and by powerful groups in Indian society. The University Education Commission (1948–1949) led by the philosopher Sarvepalli Radhakrishnan opined that "*no student should be allowed to take a degree who does not acquire the ability to read with facility and understanding works of English authors.*" This trend of privileging English and consciously or unwittingly de-privileging the Indian languages has continued nearly unabated in the last 70 years of independent India. Independent India continues to be mentally dependent on the English language, the new Brahminical thread that adorns and binds India. The foreign/world/international language—English in the most part, with Russian emerging for a couple of decades during the Cold War—does not cease to hypnotize the power classes of India. Even so, the spread of English language remains extremely limited. In 2006–2009, the National Knowledge Commission (NKC) thought that not even 2% Indians had any substantive facility with English—this almost two centuries after Macaulay, Bentinck, and the school book societies of Calcutta and Bombay! While there has been half-baked policy pushes toward the use of Indian languages in higher education, only NKC gives a distinct push toward translation of educational texts into Indian languages. And even that thrust has not gone much farther into colleges and universities. In the elite centers of higher learning, I doubt whether in a whole year we have ten PhDs in each of the natural and social sciences written in languages other than English or even less that important scholarly and scientific books of world repute written in German, French, or English find their way into Indian languages through translations or that college and university teachers are able to explain intricate and complex concepts in full measure in any Indian language.

The power of English captures even the social change imagination from colonial-era scientist S.C. Chuckerbutty to contemporary Dalit intellectual Chanderbhan Prasad and a variety of modernizers. Never mind that for 200 years, this "modern" language of power has failed to modernize either the Indian university or its science or its humanities or its social sciences. All this power language has done is to create islands which a class self-proclaims as centers of excellence. In addition and in intimate linkage to these islands, it has given India islands of opulence and a continent of malnutrition, poor education, low health and hygiene, and fear and awe of a power called English.

Power Institutions: Colonial University and Indian Nationalism

Colonialism and its Indian beneficiaries institutionalized English as the language of power and ascribed power to the English/Western university. The colonial university and the higher education it embodied took shape as an institution of power in the second half of nineteenth century and continued in full force till independence in 1947. Like English, its power too has remained undiminished in post-1947 India, and its character remains nearly the same as in the colonial period. The university and higher education universe played a key role in responses to colonialism and in the development of Indian nationalism. It was India's universities and its university educated who fashioned Pakistani nationalism and Indian nationalism in late nineteenth century and in the first half of twentieth century. While AMU was a hub of the growth of Pakistani nationalism in 1920s and 1930s India, colleges such as Presidency and universities of Calcutta, Bombay, Allahabad, and Madras formed the intellectual hinterland of Indian nationalism. Though Gandhi took Indian nationalism far beyond the confines of the colonial Indian university and the English-educated, the university class retained the functional control of nationalist movement and impinged its class power efficiently at independence and after. For the university, the language of education was English while the language of politics evolved from colonialism to nationalism. English, university, and nationalism—a triad of power—phased out colonial rule. But true to Macaulay's thought, English and British/European knowledge as also the systems of control outlived colonial rule; their intrinsic power remains nearly undiminished 70 years after independence.

There were attempts to fashion a non-colonized education in the first half of twentieth century. Tagore's educational institutions in Santiniketan and Sriniketan in Bengal and Jamia Milia Islamia in north India glow as examples where Indian thought and practice leaders tried to develop an educational universe that challenged colonial education and strived to create an education of freedom, civilizational harmony, and peace. But these moments of luminous institutional education did not grip the imagination of the larger sections of colonized university-educated Indians, nor could these institutions light the passion of freedom and peace in the vast majority of the population. The light of a Tagore or a Gandhi or a Gandhian like Zakir Hussain could not find effective flame-bearers in the colonized minds of the bearers of Indian or Pakistani nationalism. An alien language, an alien institutional transplant, and an alien political technology inaugurated a new power structure in India as colonialism came to an end.

World Powers, Science as Power, and Little or not so Little Power of People

Britain exited India, its power too receded on the world stage. Decolonization in large parts of Asia and Africa meant the colonial powers of France and Britain became weaker. The post-1945 world saw the emergence of two rival world powers, America and Soviet Russia. Their rivalry and competing economic ideologies of capitalism and socialism greatly influenced Indian politicians, policymakers, and higher education universe. While American help actively shaped the development of a number of IITs and IIMs, Russians too were not left behind in their active partnership with building and expanding India's scientific and technological base. Americans helped India in industrial agriculture; Russians lent their expertise in building steel plants and factories to produce machines. With command of English, of nation, and of the state, Prime Minister Nehru firmly espoused the development of these large infrastructure projects which he called "commanding heights of economy." And he and his policy advisers built the IITs and IIMs which I call the commanding heights of education.

Indian elite was armed with English and nationalism, it had inherited a state system with university as a key player in that system; now, it aspired to science, especially high science and higher technology.

The IITs were designed to be the new homes of technology and of science; the IIMs were designed so as to disseminate the products of technology to markets and to manage industrial and commercial organizations. What the new world powers did to the Indian elite and institutionally educated middle-class imagination was to entrench veneration for science, even more for technology than for science. Managing its relationship with the world powers, Indian power elite equipped itself and its associate classes with the power of science and the technology that science generated. The IITs, the IIMs, and major universities as envisioned in the EC (1964–1966) formed this commanding height of education. The power elite in command of the state and the nation framed policy and politics to create the commanding heights of education in order to complement commanding heights of economy. The immediate post-independence thrust toward a humanistic and democratic higher education with rural universities at the core of educational planning, articulated in UEC, fell by the wayside. A culture and economy of command nurtured a command education meant to keep the gates of institutional education closed for the largest sections of population, a world that has often been referred to as Bharat in recent years. India's commanding heights of economy and of education closed the gates of education and prosperity for Bharat.

By mid-1980s, India could also feel that it was far from being a scientific and technological powerhouse, the charms of Soviet big industry had also receded, and the pressure of the electorate was pushing for greater democracy in education and development. The National Policy on Education (NPE) (1986–1992) reflected this reality check. Instead of major and metropolitan universities, we hear of open universities for the first time, and we also see a much-needed push toward women's education and the effort to open up university education for larger numbers of lower-caste population. The late 70s and 80s also see half-baked attempts at enhancing the possibilities of use of languages other than English in education. These do not go far enough and, in some instances, defeat the purpose of greater educational opportunities for largest section of population. Nonetheless, the late 1980s and early 1990s are a time for greater educational democracy, not to mention the extension of reservation of seats for OBCs in higher education institutions.

At the time that nerve centers of power were getting more widespread across the length and breadth of India and the Soviet Union collapsed and the Berlin Wall fell, it was in those very years that the ideas of less government interference and more private investment in economy was gaining ground in the Western world. Reaganomics championed greater private role in capitalism, and the socialist Soviet Union became a thing of the past. The post-1991 world in India got enamored with liberalization, privatization, and globalization. The push for democratic higher education in the mid and late 1980s receded in the 1990s. Private higher education became the new mantra. In 2000 during Prime Minister Vajpayee's tenure, industrialists Mukesh Ambani and Kumar Mangalam Birla headed a committee on education and that gave a distinct push toward private universities. From the philosopher Radhakrishnan chairing UEC to physics professor Kothari leading EC to private industrialists at the helm of education committee, the change in Indian elite perceptions was loud and clear.

In 2006–2009, NKC and, in 2008–2009, the CARHE analyzed Indian higher education in substantive detail. Both the policy advisory groups alerted the nation to the crisis in higher education. Through a variety of measures, they advocated how higher education could be revitalized. NKC laid great stress on the importance of making translations of scientific and educational texts available in all major Indian languages, CARHE urged IITs to step out into the real world, and the policy makers sounded a clear alarm that Indian higher education and universities must sit up before it is too late. In spite of their detailed analysis and some appropriate recommendations, the pattern of India planning for Bharat continued. An idea of decentralized policymaking was absent. And like their predecessors such as Kothari, they too laid stress on creation of 50 "national" universities and centers of excellence. The elite obsession in higher education policy planning did not quite fade away. Yet from their analysis and recommendations, it was evident that the post-1991 thrust on private higher education in an era of economic privatization and globalization was far from unproblematic. To the contrary, higher education was clearly on a downward slope even though there was a modest increase in gross enrolment ratio (GER).

My survey of higher education policy from 1947 till now tells me that the idea world keeps moving between two ends of a pendulum, namely, between elite consolidation and educational democracy. For the most part, elite-centric higher education has dominated colonized India's and independent India's policy environment and policy thinking. Occasionally with the influence of Gandhian leadership of the freedom struggle, and of Ambedkar's push toward social justice, we find educational democracy finding prominence in policy thinking; UEC (1948–1949) remains a bright example. Educational democracy returns to the policy table again in late 1980s but is again elbowed out by the forces of privatization and economic globalization that have ruled Indian policy environment from the early 1990s till today. While Anglophone techno-savvy upper-caste upper- and middle-class India has profited from this policy environment—even that gain is not without its shortcomings—three-quarters or more of the population, the world called Bharat, has been denied of its political right to higher/tertiary education. The self-seeking and myopic policy thinking of the university educated is to blame for this to a great extent, but not exclusively. The political and social movements that have aspired to change the status quo have also not been able to assert an accurate set of policy recommendations. A new language of politics and policy alone can change this English-nation-class/caste-science-techno-modernity and its habitat—the Indian university. For now, we can say, here I borrow a phrase from Mohammed Yunus of Bangladesh's Grameen Bank fame, Indian higher education could be a banyan tree but elite policy has made it a bonsai.

Oppressive Power of Policy, Undemocratic Polity

An elitist policy creates commanding heights of education. The popular aspiration, embedded in large part of the population, is to get the advantage of these commanding heights. Reservation of seats for backward sections of society, enforced by the forces of political democracy, ensures that the elite institutions in technology, medicine, law, and various professional disciplines are open to students from underprivileged sections. The enormous pull of the elite institutions has resulted in an unhealthy race to get into these places. Coaching centers that train students to "crack" the competitive exams that are the gatekeepers to these institutions have become a thriving business; the companies could well get listed on the Bombay Stock Exchange. For less than a 100 seats to the AIIMS in Delhi, the number of students who sit for the entrance test in a year is 1 million! A sickening culture of examinations has become all pervasive, and the cost to the mental health of young Indians and their families is not even measured. Alongside this disease comes another social deformity. Young people who enter these centers of commanding heights, if they happen to be from Dalit or other underprivileged sections, then they are exposed to discrimination in campus life. That has resulted in student suicides, and the number of such cases seems to be rising in the last two decades. Several young people are also elbowed out by the culture of upper-caste/class cultural power in these institutions; their educational aspirations die into dark silence.

The discrimination is not only along caste lines but gender also forms an axis of discrimination. In many instances, women do not get the enabling environment that is necessary to move ahead in educational and professional careers. Physiological disabilities form yet another axis of discrimination. While there are oppressive policy and a pattern of social discrimination, there is also bureaucratic power. Often, higher education institutions and the teachers who work in these places are within a hierarchy of power; in many instances, the power of an educational administrator or an administrative body results in an oppressive climate. Instead of governing institutions, the trend is to control them. In all of this, the oppressive power of elitist policy is particularly disturbing. As I said earlier, here is a clear case how a nation's ill-thought policy—self-inflicted injuries—to use a phrase of scientist Sabyasachi Bhattacharya, gives rise to a bonsai nation.

What happens to the university in a bonsai nation? Parochial university, an idea introduced by Susan and Lloyd Rudolph in 1970s, was a formulation that when traditional institutions like caste became more cosmopolitan in an era of political and economic mobility, cosmopolitan institutions such as university started becoming parochial. I have argued in "Class Struggles in Classrooms" that there were serious limitations to the cosmopolitan character of university even in the early years of independent India. Nonetheless, it is true that the limited expansion in student numbers and the journey of higher education from the metropolis to the moffusil made the university more parochial. As higher education brought greater numbers into its fold and as, one could argue, it became more open to a large section of society, it started losing its international orientation and its cosmopolitanism. While there is merit in this argument, this characterizes only one half of the phenomenon. The Rudolphs also ask: Could the Indian university then create knowledge that was sensitive to local needs; could the local get integrated into knowledge? Nearly 40 years later, a committee to look into higher education led by Indian academics thought the same; Indian university has utterly neglected the process of even attempting to integrate local environment into knowledge creation, and I will add, to teaching. As I have argued in "Elite Institutions, Dismal Development," Indian university is caught in a black shoe syndrome; its core created in the British colonial structure remains unreformed. Cosmetic changes keep changing the shine every now and again but the core of knowledge universe and processes of teaching remain frozen in the colonial and colonized university. Indian academics are fond of the word autonomy, while there is a case of administrative autonomy, the greater and more urgent need of autonomy is the unshackling of Indian higher education from the oppressive power of colonial university and its parochial avatar. Freedom in the university will also lead to a flowering of the bonsai nation into a banyan tree of knowledge and economic prosperity for a billion plus civilization.

Educational Democracy and Developmental Futures

In the scholarship centering on higher education, some scholars focus on numbers while others look at the endemic malaise in the system of Indian higher education. GER, that is, the percentage of population of college-going age, who actually enroll in tertiary education, is important, and so is the quality of educational outcome/experience of students. As a scientist has observed, only throwing money or increasing numbers of institutions will not solve the problem. Endemic features such as caste/class biases need to be addressed urgently. Public policy cannot change in short or even in the medium term the long processes of culture that form a people's "habits of the heart." However, policy can give signals in the right direction. To begin with, the four-tier hierarchy in higher education can be changed to a two-tier system; research centers can all become universities and offer masters-level courses; and vocational/skills education can be brought into undergraduate colleges so that the stigmatization of this sector ends once and for all. The mentality of caste and of hierarchy is the central malaise that plagues higher education and India. Its tentacle spreads to the languages. A robust and dynamic translation program must be initiated to transform at least a dozen Indian languages into languages of natural and health sciences, technology, business, and social sciences. Caste and class are intermeshed, there are patterns of the mind, and there is a language in which money speaks. The high levels of funding to IITs and IIMs have to freeze at current levels. If India wants to aspire for any target of "Viswajeet" or winning the world, let the money be evenly spread out to the entire higher education sector consisting 20,000 institutions, rather than giving to a handful of elite ones. The way to promote excellence is not to create elite clubs. Unlike some advanced economies, India has scarce little money available for innovative ideas/projects. It is urgent to devise systems where money should be disbursed through competitive procedures and not handed out as an institutional birthright. There is a constant talk of becoming a world power or conquering the world in the Indian elite and media world. There is a national celebration for rocket launches, etc. but there is no national shame or disgrace at periodic train accidents, at student suicides, at farmer suicides, at floods every other year with the great loss of life and livelihood, at malnutrition, at illiteracy, and at environmental degradation. This myopia needs to be replaced by a saner democratic humane perspective of development values. Disciplines and course contents need to be rethought, so too the regime of disciplines; the push needs to be both local and international with a multi-polar power/knowledge world in context, and planetary with a planet stretched to its limits. When the educative functions of society start a new educative process, only then will the learning and development outcomes of university undergo a radical shift. A democratic change in the policy environment alone can lead to educational democracy and meaningful development for both India and Bharat, whose development has been long overdue.

Bibliography

Government Commission Reports / Policy Documents

Education Commission. 1970. *Education and National Development: Report of the Education Commission (EC)*. New Delhi: NCERT

Ministry of Human Resources Development. 1992. *National Policy on Education 1986—Programme on Action 1992 (NPE)*. New Delhi: Government of India.

Ministry of Human Resources Development. 2010. *Report of Committee to Advise on the Renovation and Rejuvenation of Higher Education (CARHE)*. New Delhi: Government of India.

National Knowledge Commission. 2009. *National Knowledge Commission—Report to the Nation (NKC)*. New Delhi.

Prime Minister's Council on Trade and Industry. 2000. *Report on A Policy Framework for Reforms in Education (PFRE)*. New Delhi: Government of India.

University Education Commission. 1950. *Report of the University Education Commission (UEC)*. New Delhi: Government of India.

Books / Articles / Essays

Agarwal, Pawan (ed.). 2012. *A Half-Century of Indian Higher Education: Essays by Philip G.* Altbach New Delhi: Sage Publications.

Altbach, Philip G. 1993. Gigantic Peripheries: India and China in World Knowledge System. *Economic and Political Weekly* 28 (24): 1220–1225.

Ambedkar, B.R. 1936. *Annihilation of Caste*. Bombay. ccnmtl.columbia.edu/projects/mmt/ambedkar/web/readings/aoc_print_2004.pdf.

S. Roy Chowdhury, *Politics, Policy and Higher Education in India*,
DOI 10.1007/978-981-10-5056-5

Barra, Joseph. 1998. Colonialism and Educational Fragmentation in India. In Bhattacharya 1998a.

Basu, Aparna. 1974. *The Growth of Education and Political Development in India, 1898–1920*. New Delhi: Oxford University Press.

Basu, Aparna. 1982. Education of Civil Servants during the Company Period. *Essays in the History of Indian Education*. New Delhi: Concept.

Basu, Aparna. 1982. *Essays in the History of Indian Education*. New Delhi: Concept Publishing Company.

Bhattacharjee, Manash. 2016. The Clarity of a Suicide Note. *The Hindu*. http://www.thehindu.com/opinion/op-ed/The-clarity-of-a-suicide-note/article14017737.ece.

Bhattacharya, Abhijit. 2010. Mismanagement of Indian Management Education. *Economic and Political Weekly* 45 (24): 14–17.

Bhattacharya, Sabyasachi. (ed.). 1998. *The Contested Terrain: Perspectives on Education in India*. New Delhi: Orient Longman.

Bhattacharya, Sabyasachi. 1998. The Contested Terrain of Education. In Bhattacharya 1998a.

Bhattacharya, Sabyasachi. 2011. Indian Science Today: An Indigenously Crafted Crisis. *Social Research* 78 (1): 255–280.

Bhokta, Naresh Prasad. 1998. Marginalisation of Popular Languages and Growth of Sectarian Education in Colonial India. In Bhattacharya 1998a.

Bourdieu, Pierre, and Jean-Claude Passeron. 1990. *Reproduction in Education, Society and Culture*. London: Sage Publications.

Broadfoot, Patricia, et al. (eds.). 1981. *Politics and Educational Change: An International Survey*. London: Croom Helm.

Chari, Mridula. 2016. Over 50 years ago, Bengal's chief engineer predicted that the Farakka dam would flood Bihar. *Scroll* https://scroll.in/a/827254.

Chatterjee, Partha. 2016. Freedom of Speech in the University. *Economic and Political Weekly* 51 (11): 35–37.

Chopra, Ritika. 2016. IITs Estimate It Will Cost Rs 22,000 Crore To Improve Global Rankings. *The Indian Express*, November 15. http://indianexpress.com/article/education/proposals-submitted-to-govt-iits-estimate-cost-of-improving-global-rankings-rs-22000-crore-4375827/.

Chowdhury, Rekha. 2008. Autonomy and Dignity of Teachers. *Seminar*, 587: 48–51.

Clotfelter, Charles T. (ed.). 2010. *American Universities in A Global Market*. Chicago: University of Chicago Press.

Commission on National Education. 1959. *Report of the Commission on National Education*. Islamabad: Government of Pakistan.

Dasgupta, Uma. 1998. Santiniketan: The School of A Poet. In Hasan 1998a.

Dasgupta, Uma (ed.). 2009. *The Oxford India Tagore: Selected Writings on Education and Nationalism*. New Delhi: Oxford University Press.

D'mello, Bernard. 1999. Management Education. *Economic and Political Weekly* 34 (48): M169–M176.

Dreze, Jean, and Amartya Sen. 2011. Putting Growth In Its Place. *Outlook*, 14 November, 2011. https://www.outlookindia.com/magazine/story/putting-growth-in-its-place/278843.

EPW Editorial. 2016. Killing Children of the Middle Class. *Economic and Political Weekly* 51 (2): 7–8.

Express Web Desk. 2016. Union Budget 2016: Mixed Reaction From Education Sector. *The Indian Express*, March 1. http://indianexpress.com/article/education/union-budget-2016-education-sector-analysis/.

Ghosh, Swati, and Ashok Sarkar. 2015. *Kabir pathshala: pathabhavan o sikshasatrer itihas*. Calcutta: Signet Press.

Gould, Harold. 1972. Educational Structures and Political Processes in Faizabad District, Uttar Pradesh. In Rudolph and Rudolph 1972a.

Guha, Ramachandra. 2009. The Rise and Fall of the Bilingual Intellectual. *Economic and Political Weekly* 44 (33): 36–42.

Hasan, Mushirul (ed.). 1998. *Knowledge, Power & Politics: Educational Institutions in India*. New Delhi: Roli Books.

Hasan, Mushirul. 1998. Negotiating with Its Past and Present: The Changing Profile of the Aligarh Muslim University. In Hasan 1998a.

Jangam, Chinnaiah. 2015. Politics of Identity and the Project of Writing History in Postcolonial India: A Dalit Critique. *Economic and Political Weekly* 50 (40): 63–70.

Jeffrey, Craig. 2010. Timepass: Youth, Class, and Time Among Unemployed Young Men in India. *American Ethnologist* 37 (3): 465–481.

Kapur, Devesh, and Pratap Bhanu Mehta. 2004. *Indian Higher Education Reform: From Half-baked Socialism to Half-baked Capitalism*. Cambridge, MA: Harvard Center for International Development. https://www.hks.harvard.edu/centers/cid/publications/faculty-working-papers/cid-working-paper-no.-108.

Kapur, Devesh. 2010. Indian Higher Education. In Clotfelter.

King, Robert D. 1997. *Nehru and the Language Politics of India*. New Delhi: Oxford University Press.

Kumar, Deepak. 1998. Educational Ideas of Bengali Scientists from 1850 to 1920. In Bhattacharya 1998a.

Kumar, Krishna. 1991. *Political Agenda of Education—A study of Colonialist and Nationalist Ideals*. New Delhi: Sage Publications.

Kumar, Vivek. 2016. How Egalitarian is Indian Sociology? *Economic and Political Weekly* 51 (25): 150–151.

Mandal, Mohitosh. 2016. Ami dalit. *Ananda bazaar patrika*. http://www.anandabazar.com/supplementary/rabibashoriyo/rabibasariyo-cover-story-on-dalit-1.291430#.

Mehta, Mona G., and Raghubir Sharan. 2016. IITs and the Project of Indian Democracy. *Economic and Political Weekly* 51 (11): 12–14.

Mukhopadhyay, Partha. 2008. Learning to Work. *Seminar*, 587: 52–57.

Nandy, Ashis. 1994. *The Illegitimacy of Nationalism—Rabindranath Tagore and the Politics of Self.* New Delhi: Oxford University Press.

Narain, Iqbal. 1972. Rural Local Politics and Primary School Management. In Rudolph and Rudolph 1972a.

Pandey, Gyanendra. 2016. Dreaming in English. *Economic and Political Weekly* 51 (16): 56–62.

Rajivlochan, M. 2008. Reforming Education for India, from England. *Seminar*, 587: 39–42.

Raza, Moonis. 1990. *Education, Development & Society.* New Delhi: Vikas Publishing House.

Roy Chowdhury, Sunandan. 2013. *Uchchho shikshar babu-brittanto: 45 lokkho shikshito bekar! Ei samay*, 3 April 2013.

Roy Chowdhury, Sunandan. 2014. Monster Anglopolis. *Planet—The Welsh Internationalist*, 216: 54–61.

Rudolph, Susanne H., and Lloyd I. Rudolph (eds.). 1972. *Education and Politics in India: Studies in Organization, Society, and Policy.* New Delhi: Oxford University Press.

Rudolph, Susanne H., and Lloyd I. Rudolph. 1972. The Political System and the Educational System: An Analysis of Their Interaction. In Rudolph and Rudolph 1972a.

Rushdie, Salman. 2012. *Joseph Anton: A Memoir.* London: Jonathan Cape.

Sadgopal, Anil. 2016. Skill India or Deskilling India: An Agenda for Exclusion. *Economic and Political Weekly*, 51 (35): 33–37.

Sarkar, Sumit. 1984. *Modern India 1885–1947.* New Delhi: Macmillan.

Sengupta, Nirmal. 1999. A Buzzword Named Development. *The Hindu.* http://www.narmada.org/archive/hindu/files/hindu.19990831.05312524.htm.

Sloss, Robert. 1981. Ideology and Politics in Chinese Education. In Broadfoot.

Tagore, Rabindranath. 1920. *Nationalism* (Reprint). London: Macmillan (Original 1917 edition published by Book Club of California, San Francisco).

Tagore, Rabindranath. 1941. *Crisis in Civilisation.* Calcutta: Viswa Bharati.

Talib, Mohammad. 1998. Jamia Milia Islamia: Career of Azad Talim. In Hasan 1998a.

The Hindu Special Correspondent. 2006. Upper Castes Dominate National Media, Says Survey in Delhi. *The Hindu*, June 5, 2016. http://www.thehindu.com/todays-paper/tp-national/upper-castes-dominate-national-media-says-survey-in-delhi/article3115113.ece.

Vishnoi, Anubhuti. 2016. MHRD's New Project Vishwajeet Aims to Put IIT in Top League of Global Rankings. *Economic Times*, August 10. http://

economictimes.indiatimes.com/industry/services/education/mhrds-new-project-vishwajeet-aims-to-put-iit-in-top-league-of-global-rankings/articleshow/53626151.cms.

Watson, Keith. 1981. Higher Education and Political Change in Thailand. In Broadfoot.

Zachariah, B., S.R. Chakraborti, and R.K. Ray. 1998. Presidency College, Calcutta: An Unfinished History. In Hasan 1998a.

INDEX

S. Roy Chowdhury, *Politics, Policy and Higher Education in India*,
DOI 10.1007/978-981-10-5056-5

P

Q

R

CPSIA information can be obtained
at www.ICGtesting.com
Printed in the USA
BVOW06*0247120917
494629BV00008B/74/P

9 789811 050558